Angel First Aid

for Success

Sue Storm
The Angel Lady

©*Angelight Productions,* 2002

Designed by Steve Krupowicz

Cover art by Susan V. Holton

Photograph by Stuart Pearson

Consulting by Conni M. Pluchino

Manufactured in the United States of America

Second in a Series

ISBN 0-9675291-1-5

The Angel Lady™ is a trademark of
Angelight Productions

Message from Archangel Michael

Angel First Aid, Rx for Success *is meant to provide guidance for those individuals seeking their purpose in life. All of us from the Angelic Realm offer genuine wisdom and support as a prescription for success.*

Dedication

To my daughter, Rochelle, who inspires me to write. She has contributed to my success by providing her encouragement and support throughout the years.

Acknowledgments

Writing this book has been a labor of love for so many people. It could not have been accomplished without the dedicated efforts of my gifted "Angel Assistants"—Conni Pluchino, Mary Jo Porter, Mariann Murphy, and Richard Dilworth.

Others who have contributed to the success of *Angel First Aid* are Alan Fox, Michelle Farina, Sally Morrocco, Marty Turck, Lucian Kaminsky, Nancy Banaszak, Kathy Sparrow, Betty Work, Dawna Page, Denice Gierach, Tom Martin, and Debbie Manning.

Sincere appreciation to my family, the Belkins, for their continual support: Major and Anita; Bernie and Tiki; Steve and Joan; Julie, Amy, Hadar, Rinat, and Michael. Also, thanks to Hannah Storm; my uncle, Mel Dean; aunt, Jessie Belkin; cousins, Andrea Belkin, Sheila and Steve Cohen, and Joan Bogart.

Credit is given to the friends and clients whose encouragement has been particularly heartwarming: Jill and Tom Lueken, Ruth Kalas, Thelma Fastner, Don O'Neill, Martin Minney, Irena Lewkowicz, Kayrita Anderson, Ed Moline, Cindy Wheeler, Evelyn Rice, Amy Wayton, David Wells, Ann Rhode, and Cheryl Maraffio.

Much gratitude is also extended to those who have served as my mentors throughout the years: Anne Simon-Wolf, Carol Canova,

Sara Allen, Darla Engelmann, Annie Hall, Genevieve Paulson, Linda Howe, and Alice Umbach. They all played a major role in helping me to achieve my life's purpose.

Acknowledgments also include: Kelley Wardzala, Borders Books and Music; Diane Simowski, Barnes & Noble Booksellers; Rose George, Radio and TV Interview Report; Jeffrey Dauler, Guest Exchange; and Mayor George Pradel (Naperville, Illinois).

Much appreciation is offered to those in the media: Stewart Bailey, Mike Murphy, Steve McCoy, Vikki Locke, Mike Morgan, Jack Olson, Shawn Novatt, Megan Butterly, and Oprah Winfrey, who lives my dream of being able to help people.

Special thanks to God, "My Little Man," and the Angels for, in truth, the *Angel First Aid* series is their work.

Table of Contents

The Angel Lady

My first encounter with Angelic intervention took place in East Grand Rapids, Michigan. At eighteen months of age, wrapped up in my blankets almost to the point of suffocation, I had a near-death experience. However, Guardian Angels flying overhead provided comfort and made sure that I was saved. On my fourth birthday, a special guidance in the form of a voice I called "My Little Man" started offering me good advice. He disclosed what would take place in the future and told me how to make things happen.

Years later, in Naperville, Illinois, an extraordinary event occurred that changed the course of my life. While I was at work, the ceiling seemed to open and a booming voice called out, "Sue, you have to help people!" My body resonated with this powerful command. I responded immediately: "Yes, God, what do you want me to do?" The next few years were exciting as my purpose became apparent. I followed God's directive to "help people" by developing a career as a prosperity consultant. In this way, I could share my definition of genuine prosperity—the achievement of success in every aspect of one's life.

In 1996, My Little Man told me to "make a writing room." The divine plan was for Barbara Mark and Trudy Griswold, authors of *Angelspeake*, to use this area for editing their second book. While the three of us collaborated, these special women answered many questions. Their most surprising revelation was that My Little Man is Archangel Michael! He is the one who has been guiding me all along toward making Angels and prosperity my life's work.

Angels Among Us

*C*elestial Beings act as the messengers of God and were created specifically to provide support, guidance, and protection. Constantly present, they possess boundless energy and desire to be of service to all mankind. Three Angels are assigned to each newborn. These personal Guardians render care and assist their charges throughout their lives. Advice that comes from "The Messengers" helps everyone to be more successful.

All monotheistic religions of the world acknowledge the existence of Angels. Throughout history, they have appeared in the writings and symbols of Christianity, Judaism, Islam, and many of the other spiritual traditions. While the presence of Angels is recognized in most religions, it is not necessary to have a particular affiliation to receive their support.

Four significant and especially powerful Celestial Beings known as "Archangels" take care of humanity. They have a broad range of responsibility and offer assistance to people. The Guardian Angels differ from the Archangels in that their attention is focused on the individuals they were chosen to help.

Angel Specialists have been given a designated area of expertise so people can call upon the Angel best suited to handle each situation. Some of them assume human form for a period of time to serve a definite purpose and are referred to as "Physical Angels."

Those who are deceased can act as Guardian Angels and return to Earth temporarily. Often, their arrival is evidenced by a symbol or sign, such as a familiar fragrance or presence in a dream. Leaving once the specific mission has been completed, they reappear when circumstances warrant.

Celestial Beings will be instantly dispatched to assist humanity in any way possible. Angels are always available to help improve the environment and perpetuate world peace. There is no limit to what they can do!

How to Use This Book

*A*ngel First Aid, Rx for Success is a guide to seeking the counsel of Guardian Angels and reaping the benefit of their great wisdom. By communicating with Celestial Beings, you can enrich your life. Practicing the exercises, referred to as "remedies," helps individuals improve their physical, mental, and spiritual as well as financial well-being. Connecting with the Angelic Realm is a way for you to feel continually supported and blessed. *Angel First Aid,* as a reference or handbook, produces a cumulative effect that accelerates personal growth.

This book also offers suggestions for making success an everyday reality. Gaining direction through performing the techniques can result in dramatic, constructive change. Consider all remedies as "recipes" from an Angelic cookbook. Individually and combined, they will enhance progress. When used regularly, these exercises become valuable tools for success.

Miracle Stories are special, personal accounts from those people whose lives have been touched by Celestial Beings. Each features an amazing encounter that had a profound impact. These episodes illustrate the benevolence of the Angelic Realm.

Steps to Success is a professional review of Sue Storm's career and business experience. The Angel Lady shares her Steps to Success, along with ideas to uncover clues from childhood for identifying one's life purpose.

Each of the chapters, *Focus, Organization, Relaxation, Strength, Understanding, Creativity, Confidence, Energy, and Support,* as well as *Success,* is filled with useful information and features:

Affirmations - Declarative statements that will produce positive effects on the mind, body, and spirit.

Consultation - Introduction from one Angel Specialist offering guidance with a fresh outlook.

Angel Specialists - A partial listing of Celestial Beings highlighting their particular areas of focus.

Case Study - Real-life story which incorporates Angel First Aid Techniques and Steps to Success.

Remedies - Exercises and activities that promote well-being, along with dosages for best results.

Preventative Medicine - Guidelines for using remedies as an extended maintenance program.

Success Questions - Queries pertaining to careers, with Angel Specialists and Primary Remedies.

Second Opinion - Suggestions for achieving prosperity from an already successful professional.

Miracle Story - One person's Angelic encounter, along with the dramatic effect experienced.

6

Prescription for Success provides insight and advice contributed by prosperous individuals in a variety of fields. These participants were selected because their recommendations or proven methods of performance originate from a spiritual perspective.

Glossary of Angels, a "Who's Who" for the Angelic Realm, offers a convenient alphabetical listing that describes each Angel's field of expertise. Many Celestial Beings not mentioned in the chapters are cited in the glossary.

Keys to Success is an index that functions as an integral part of the book. It can be used to locate remedies by referencing keywords. Consulting this helpful guide assists with identifying the exercises or techniques that will be most beneficial in a given circumstance.

For Best Results

Take time to develop ongoing relationships with all your Angels. Invite them to be participants in every facet of your life. Enlisting celestial support becomes easier with frequent practice. Speak to The Messengers in the same way you would converse with one of your friends; making an Angel a confidante can be very rewarding. Share ideas, desires, and dreams to establish a closer bond.

Celestial Beings prefer to be addressed personally, so learn your Angels' names to make more direct contact. One of the best ways for individuals to identify their Archangels or Guardian Angels is to write or say aloud, "Angel, what is your name?" Then sit quietly and listen for the response.

Guardian Angels are accessible to humans at any time. They make their presence evident through feelings, symbols, and dreams. A relaxed state of mind is conducive to receiving clear information. Messages will be conveyed so that the recipient sees, hears, or is touched by the Angels.

Insight offered by an Angel can be easily recognized because of the feelings of warmth that it elicits. Celestial Beings will converse in the language that is clearly understood. To initiate contact, prepare your questions or requests in advance being as detailed as possible. Keep a private journal that contains the divine advice you receive for future reference.

Affirmations also enhance effectiveness of the remedies and work by focusing on the positive. The declarative statements create ideal outcomes. When formulating your own, use *I am*... or *I have*... to begin each sentence. Repetition increases potency, so recite these statements often.

Results are improved by generating enthusiasm for each scenario visualized in the various exercises. If directed, hold the feeling or sensation for at least one minute. The benefits experienced will be imprinted in the cells of your body. Loosen up by stretching after completing an Angel First Aid Technique.

Perform the remedies when it is most convenient, doing your best to follow directions as presented. If modification is required due to circumstances—business travel, time constraints, or inconvenient location—then use your initiative to adapt or change the suggested methods. Guardian Angels respond based on personal intentions that focus on making progress.

Even though Angels are involved, some remedies will take time to work. Be patient and persevere. When communicating, practice is advisable to differentiate between your own ideas and those from an Angelic source. However, conversation flows freely once this skill has been mastered.

Angel First Aid Techniques have been performed by thousands of individuals, resulting in greater joy, understanding, happiness, and fulfillment. Believe in Angelic guidance and trust in the process to further your own success.

Miracle Stories

*H*undreds of Angel stories have come to the attention of The Angel Lady during speaking engagements, media interviews, and individual sessions. People's lives are often touched and transformed through these encounters. Although circumstances vary, there is a common theme—Angels are always available to provide guidance, protection, and support for their charges.

Angels on Duty

Several years ago, at a Professional Speakers Bureau showcase, J.J., a famous Chicago detective, told me about his brush with death while on duty. An armed suspect had fled down an alley and J.J. was in close pursuit. Suddenly, the offender turned and fired at the detective's chest. An obvious hole right in the back of J.J.'s unbuttoned raincoat verified how close to him the bullet had actually come. "The Angels must have moved either me or the bullet!" he exclaimed, shaking his head in wonderment.

At this point, Wayne, another featured speaker, joined our conversation. Familiar with the subject of Angels, he was eager to reveal his own Angelic story. Having visited with some friends after singing the national anthem at the Chicago Stadium, Wayne was preparing for the long drive home. As he turned the key in the ignition, a bullet burst through the window and tore into his throat. A short time later, while waiting for an ambulance, he thought, "I hope my Guardian Angel is not on vacation."

Wayne's recovery was an amazing miracle. I recently heard him singing "The Star-Spangled Banner." There is no doubt that his Guardian Angel was on duty that day!

Inspiration Plus

Having experienced Angelic intervention in her youth, Diana was eager to resume contact. During a telephone consultation with me, she expressed a desire to thank her father's Guardian Angels and then related this heartwarming story.

Although he owned the company, Dad always worked right alongside his men. Just after my eleventh birthday, he suffered life-threatening injuries in a terrible construction accident. Mom received a call from the hospital reporting that Dad was in intensive care and not expected to survive. My next memory is of sitting alone in the dark sanctuary of a church. For several hours, I wept and prayed to God and my father's Angels to save his life. We were so close; I just could not let him go. Much later I hurried home to where my whole family was waiting. They had gathered from all over to say their goodbyes.

When the phone rang the following morning, a glimmer of hope came over me. Trembling, I listened intently as my mom said, "A miracle happened last night. Your dad's vital signs have improved and he is out of danger!" God and the Guardian Angels had heard my pleas—he was still with us.

After regaining consciousness, my father remembered seeing Angels and hearing their words of encouragement. Recalling those supportive comments helped him bravely face many bumps in the road without ever complaining or losing hope. Even though Dad was paralyzed from the waist down, we were able to share another thirty years. Since his passing, family and friends continue to be inspired by my father's positive attitude.

(Read about Diana's career on page 50.)

Foggy Night

One memorable evening, Nancy discovered she was not alone on the road. Wishing to share her Angelic encounter, yet unable to get through during a radio broadcast in California, she told me about her experience via e-mail.

Many years ago when I was in high school, my friends suggested going to a movie. After the show, I drove them home, dropping Stacey off last because she lived out in the country. It was really foggy, with visibility decreasing by the minute. I pulled out of the driveway, turned the radio up loud, and headed for home.

Within minutes it became impossible to see more than a few yards beyond the headlights. Suddenly, an attractive woman appeared, waving her arms as if trying to flag me down. Getting closer, I realized that what I saw waving at me were actually large wings. Blinking repeatedly failed to clear my vision. I slammed on the brakes to keep from hitting her.

As my vehicle came to a halt, the Angel vanished and so did the fog! Only then was a huge fallen tree visible just ahead. Stunned, I sat there in complete silence for at least twenty minutes. Even the radio had shut off, although my fingers never touched the dial.

Since that night, it seems as if a Guardian Angel has always been with me. Today, working for a national retail clothing chain, I often find it necessary to be on the road to service my accounts. While traveling, I keep a watchful eye for that very special Angel in the middle of the road.

Angelic Trio

Marcia, a coordinator for Newman-Haas Racing, described this Angelic intervention after hearing me speak at a library. Reticent for years about sharing the details of this extraordinary incident, she took advantage of the opportunity afforded to divulge her own incredible story.

On a wintry night during a snowfall, with a windchill of thirty below, I left work late. As usual, I was not dressed for Chicagoland weather and the cold air caused me to shiver.

My ride home necessitated traveling through a largely undeveloped area. While on this particular stretch of road, a tire blew out, sending my car straight toward a telephone pole. Without my input, the steering wheel corrected itself, and the vehicle glided into a driveway.

Quickly recovering from the shock, I realized my awful predicament. Unfortunately, no one appeared to be home in the house directly ahead of me and the only other dwelling in view was under construction. To my surprise, a car was idling in front. Braving the cold to get help seemed my best hope. Upon reaching the front door, I opened it and yelled, "Hello, is anyone home?"

Bright moonlight shining through the framed windows clearly showed three tall figures, two females and one male, coming down the stairs. First to approach me was a young woman who seemed to be carefully reading my lips while I described my plight. She nodded in acknowledgment, then signed to her companions.

Soon, we got into their car and started back to the office using the interior light so the woman driving could see my lips in order to follow the directions. After arriving safely, I gratefully hugged the driver and was astonished to hear her say aloud, "Just don't forget us!"

Upon entering the building, I turned around for one last look. To my amazement, there was no car, no tracks in the snow—just me wondering what happened.

This episode presents a perfect example of how "Physical Angels" intercede. Celestial Beings appear as needed and vanish as soon as their mission has been completed. Marcia now felt comfortable revealing information about her Angelic intervention. Individuals sometimes suppress their encounters until they learn about similar events that have been experienced by others.

15

Steps to Success

*T*aking inventory of all previous accomplishments and experiences charts a steady course for future growth. My career as The Angel Lady encompassed a variety of unique opportunities that ultimately laid a strong foundation for Angelight Productions.

Owning a bowling supply distributorship in the Midwest area was my first entrepreneurial endeavor. Using visualization as a tool to increase sales presented a definite advantage. Managing a start-up business, cultivating customer relationships, and designing a large 4,000-item catalog were instrumental in the formation and growth of this organization.

Steps to Success:

- ♦ Be creative with advertising and marketing
- ♦ Delegate responsibility and trust the results
- ♦ Treat customers as the most important asset

Prosperity Now, a consulting firm, became the primary focus for my next business venture. Maximizing clients' potential through coaching sessions was the main objective. I developed techniques for individuals to achieve personal excellence. These enlightening exercises demonstrated how to discover talents and turn them into marketable skills.

Steps to Success:

- ♦ Identify and fulfill your life's purpose
- ♦ Learn how to manifest personal goals
- ♦ Network with a focus on your vision

As The Angel Lady, it became apparent that public speaking was my forté. For many years, I have had the privilege of presenting programs and talks to hundreds of businesses, organizations, and chambers of commerce. Experience has taught me that a speaker's best approach is to address the audience in a relaxed manner, as if engaged in a one-on-one conversation.

Steps to Success:
- Tailor the program to each individual group
- Be passionate about the topic of discussion
- Initiate a flow of energy with the audience

Writing books about Angels and helping people to understand the enormous role Celestial Beings play in our world are integral parts of my life's purpose. The many techniques selected for my books have been developed as a result of communication with the Angels and knowledge gained on my spiritual path. With divine guidance, information flows to me from various sources.

Steps to Success:
- Create a specific area for working
- Believe in the content of your book
- Keep the reader in mind at all times

Angel First Aid, Rx for Miracles began my career in publishing and was the impetus for Angelight Productions. This organization has expanded to encourage and support individuals through speaking engagements, business seminars, and coaching. *Angel First Aid, Rx for Success* is the second in a series of books that will offer an in-depth view of contemporary subjects.

Steps to Success:
- Maintain the highest standards of excellence
- Produce a product that is relevant and unique
- Work with others who share the same vision

Numerous interviews, in print and as a featured guest on hundreds of radio stations worldwide, have enabled me to interact with large audiences. Throughout call-in shows, some hosts encourage their listeners to share Angel stories; this type of program elicits a much greater response. My cable show, *A Visit with The Angel Lady*, and appearances on *Fox News, Talk Soup,* and *The Daily Show* have allowed me to extol the definitive benefits of enjoying supportive, Angelic connections.

Steps to Success:
- Give the audience useful guidance
- Be energetic, vibrant, and dynamic
- Let your enthusiasm shine through

Acquainting the public with the versatility of the Angelic Realm has evolved into a primary goal. It encompasses everything from people learning their Guardian Angels' names to online courses in personal and professional development. Some long-term goals are to produce a series of videos, compact discs, and cassette tapes on how to maximize the Angel First Aid Techniques. Additional ideas include magazine articles and a weekly radio show.

Conveying the messages of the Guardian Angels provides me with the means to make a positive impact on people's lives.

Discovering My Life's Purpose

Reflecting on talents that were evident in childhood and evaluating specific clues assist in identifying a life's purpose. This awareness can help people to determine their most successful career path. To demonstrate the process, I am sharing my own experiences.

My desire and natural ability to entertain people became evident at an early age. Reciting nursery rhymes and telling stories for family and friends at every opportunity provided the first sign that I would be a public speaker. During dance recitals, the instructor placed me in front so other four-year-olds could mimic my steps to get theirs right. That was just the beginning of many stage appearances.

As a child, I often visited my father's office and enjoyed sitting in his big chair with my feet up on the desk. Pretending to talk on the telephone, when actually communicating with "My Little Man," I visualized operating a business. This seemed an unlikely way for a little girl to play grown-up, unless it was a harbinger of the future.

During high school, a speech I gave that addressed public-versus-private prayer won praise. People said my presentation and words touched them deeply. The ability to blend thoughts and ideas when speaking or writing has proven to be an inborn gift. Throughout my teen years, I continued to perform before audiences as a dancer and as an actress in the theater.

Attending the University of Michigan thoroughly prepared me to pursue a career that combined psychology and business; however, my passion was reading the classics and writing essays about those great books. Over the years, I also studied philosophy, history, and comparative religions on my quest for enlightenment.

Reviewing the past, I saw clear indications of the way in which my life would unfold. Speaking to large audiences, writing books, and connecting with Angels are all outward expressions of my natural talents. I interpreted these clues as God's directive for me to bring the wisdom of the Angelic Realm down to Earth.

Identifying Your Life's Purpose

Designing a viable strategy for success includes discovering your life's purpose. To accomplish this goal, identify and formulate a list of the principal areas in which you already excel. These items should reflect all achievements that provide you with feelings of satisfaction. "Breathing Technique" and "Angel Scrapbook" will make it possible to get in touch with your innermost thoughts.

Breathing Technique

This exercise helps you become relaxed and receptive to guidance. While practicing the remedy, invite Robert, Angel of Balance, to be present. Standing nearby, he offers encouragement that allows you to concentrate and feel at ease. To begin the technique, inhale through the nose, visualizing the pathway for the air as it travels from your head, down your neck and spine until it reaches the base of the tailbone. Leaving some air in your tailbone, start to exhale the balance through your mouth. Repeat this especially comforting routine three times. Notice the remedy working as your own body releases its tension, resulting in a greater sense of relaxation. You will immediately feel more serene and centered in preparation for taking the next step.

Angel Scrapbook

Solicit Angelic direction for assembling a scrapbook comprised of early experiences that highlight your intrinsic talents and abilities. Put your left hand on your forehead and the right hand on the back of your head, above the neck. Focus on bringing forth memories that definitely reveal what was unique about you prior to age five. Query parents and relatives for clues that pinpoint your inherent attributes. This familial input offers clarity into areas in which you exhibited interest. Looking at the family photo albums may also be helpful. Visualize "snapshots" of yourself when you were a child engaged in favorite activities. Place these pictures in an imaginary scrapbook. Repeat this procedure, recalling the memorable events from every phase of your life. Locate any clues by asking yourself the following questions:

> What is important to me?
> What makes me special?
> What brings me peace?
> What do I like doing?
> What is easy for me?

While considering the answers, consult with Cory, Angel of Career Development, and Bettina, Angel of Creativity, to shed some light on occupations or endeavors that would best encompass the use of your distinctive talents. Once you have gained this Angelic insight and knowledge, the doors of opportunity will begin to open.

For additional benefits, create a professional review similar to that of Sue Storm's "Steps to Success." Be sure to detail your special skills and personal gifts. Note any accomplishments that document unique assets and have resulted in positive outcomes. Using this process helps to discover your career path, making life much easier and more prosperous.

AFFIRMATIONS

I am hopeful and focused.

I have a desire to succeed.

I am wise and optimistic.

I have definite goals in mind.

I am always in present time.

FOCUS

CONSULTATION

Specific goals and well-constructed plans for achieving them are essential ingredients to success. Formulating the perfect strategy to meet these objectives necessitates focus as well as clarity. Concentrating on what matters most will bring meaning to one's life and ensure growth toward prosperity.

—Gordon, Angel of Focus

ANGEL SPECIALISTS

	Archangel Michael
Caroline	Angel of Positive Thinking
Christopher	Angel of Opportunity
Cornell	Angel of Decision-Making
Jason	Angel of Organization
Lois	Angel of Clarity
Loretta	Angel of New Enterprise
Lucian	Angel of Resources
Perrie	Angel of Music
Ruth	Angel of Divine Justice
Samuel	Angel of Excellence

CASE STUDY - Finding the Right Path

The importance of an education drove Donna's career aspirations. Although this young woman tasted success at an early age, she felt something was lacking in her life.

In order to make a difference in the world, I became a CPA and a lawyer. I also earned an MBA to accommodate my clients. My focus was to always help victims of injustice who needed a strong warrior to defend them. The cases that interested me the most related to my parents' teachings of honesty and decency.

Reaching a high level of professional success by age 30 did not seem enough; I still felt compelled to discover my life's purpose. Reading about Angel First Aid Techniques in the newspaper inspired me to investigate this new opportunity. The "Angel Scrapbook" remedy revealed a scenario that included a vivid image of myself courageously protecting a new friend from a bully. This made it crystal clear to me that my purpose was to defend those who could not help themselves. I realized the benefit of integrating the values learned during childhood into my practice.

Renewed confidence garnered by following the right path, combined with input from Ruth, Angel of Divine Justice, bolsters all my professional endeavors. This allows me to champion each and every client.

Donna's Steps to Success

Look through the glasses of integrity and truth. Focus on a course of action and persist. If changes are necessary, show no hesitation in altering a plan to make it work better.

REMEDIES

Vision Statement

Most companies already have a mission statement. Smart professionals go one step further by creating a personalized vision statement. Formulate the plans that will result in success. Employ Angels as advisors to determine what can contribute most to the growth of your organization. Compose three to five affirmations that define a strategy for the company's development. Here is an example of a vision statement: *I am creating a profitable business. I have plenty of resources available. I am being rewarded for my efforts.* While contemplating a rich and fulfilling future, say these affirmations aloud three times. This is a perfect way to notify the Angels of your intention to advance.

Dosage: Daily

Goal Setting

Entrepreneurs realize the importance of setting as well as accomplishing goals. Christopher, Angel of Opportunity, provides this unique method to meet these objectives. Each morning, take a sheet of paper and write across the top: *Angel miracles fill my day.* List your goals, including details regarding the amount of money desired, time that is required, necessary materials, and anything else advisable to be successful. Add other plausible considerations that will make every day more enjoyable. Keep the paper close at hand for immediate reference. Consistent attention to all goals and a belief in miracles will produce remarkable results.

Dosage: Each day, in the morning

Brain Fog

When you are facing a major business meeting, your brain may seem a bit foggy, making it difficult to concentrate. Perform the following exercise to clear and refocus your thought processes. Visualize Lois, Angel of Clarity, hovering nearby ready to assist. Standing or sitting comfortably, extend your arms forward, palms facing down. Then, spreading your fingers, wiggle them quickly and energetically for ten seconds. Improved vision and a sense of well-being are typical reactions that signal a return of clarity. You are now feeling refreshed and more capable of tackling the items on your agenda.

Dosage: As needed

Taking Inventory

Aligning individual talents with required skills increases the potential for advancement. Practice this remedy to expand your abilities and create better opportunities. Make a list of the top five qualities that an ideal professional possesses, for example: focus, responsibility, efficiency, dependability, and promptness. Do your characteristics match this description? If not, seek assistance from Lucian, Angel of Resources, to develop the desired traits. Then, exhibit these positive attributes by thinking and acting as if you are already a success. Lucian helps you attain and perfect the qualities necessary for career growth.

Dosage: Two times a week

Baroque Beat
In order to stay alert and on top of your game, achieve focus through the use of music therapy. Play a Baroque song in the background to organize thoughts and maintain balance. This technique is effective because the tempo of 60 beats per minute synchronizes with the human brain. In addition, at the beginning of the song, tap your ring finger for at least ten seconds to the beat. Switch hands and repeat the entire process. Imagine Perrie, Angel of Music, as he accompanies you by tapping his wings. Gain increased stability and remain calm while enjoying the peaceful ambiance produced by the music.

Dosage: Regularly

PREVENTATIVE MEDICINE
- ✓ Four remedies, three times a week
- ✓ Three affirmations, two times a week

SUCCESS QUESTIONS

Can Angels contribute to a start-up business?
Hasten the progress of forming a new company by approaching celestial experts for their guidance and support. Angel Specialists infuse all entrepreneurs with an abundance of stamina to get their businesses up and running. They provide backing to obtain funds, recruit employees, and attract customers.

Angel Specialist: Loretta, Angel of New Enterprise
Primary Remedy: *Vision Statement*, page 27

Do Angels improve management skills?
Celestial Beings assist executives in developing high performance teams. By connecting with The Messengers, professionals realize clarity of thought which enhances their capability for productive management. Angels direct leaders to effect beneficial change and convey advice for employee relations.

Angel Specialist: Samuel, Angel of Excellence
Primary Remedy: *Voice Mail*, page 59

SECOND OPINION

Diana Jordan — *Associated Press Radio, award-winning host and producer of* Between the Lines *and* Portfolio. *Book reviewer for the* Portland Tribune *and* AM Northwest *(ABC Affiliate).*

Success is a quiet, calm spot deep inside; some call it faith. When I am centered and focused, the stage is set for magic to happen. A passion for books and truth has led me to follow my vision. During interviews with thousands of authors, I have received numerous special messages from these wise people. Acting as a channel for their truth to be told heightens my own sense of accomplishment. To me, good media is a tool to enlighten, educate, and entertain.

Keywords: Faith. Passion. Truth.

Miracle Story

Angelic Gratitude

Listening to an East Coast program, Heather, a photographer from New York, called for a business consultation and shared these two experiences. In her own words: "One summer, I kept my Guardian Angels working overtime."

Traveling throughout the city to take photos makes it necessary for me to cross busy streets every day. One morning, traffic seemed particularly heavy and I must have been very deep in thought because the stoplight looked green when actually it was still red. Stepping right into traffic created havoc. Drivers honked their horns and cars whizzed past. Miraculously, I reached the curb safely. The pedestrians standing nearby were astounded. One lady exclaimed, "We all saw an Angel escort you across the street."

A second incident occurred when my condo was being remodeled and friends invited me to share a penthouse apartment overlooking the Hudson River. Their guest room had a big window leading to the fire escape. One evening, while in a hurry to shoot a beautiful sunset, I crawled out the window and rushed forward. A large Angel was standing directly in front of me, pointing down. What a shock! The fire escape had a big hole in it. One more step and . . . Well, all I can say is, "Thank you, Angel."

AFFIRMATIONS

I am skilled at prioritizing.

I have everything in place.

I am adept at being prompt.

I have a choice in what I do.

I am completely organized.

ORGANIZATION

CONSULTATION

*U*sing resources wisely and prioritizing goals will make it easier to effectively meet responsibilities. Maintaining clear focus with skillful, systematic planning and time management helps individuals to be efficient and productive. With solid organization, performance is at its peak.

—Jason, Angel of Organization

ANGEL SPECIALISTS

	Archangel Gabriel
Caroline	Angel of Positive Thinking
Cornell	Angel of Decision-Making
Courtney	Angel of Responsibility
Denice	Angel of Accounting
Jessie	Angel of Deadlines
Loretta	Angel of New Enterprise
Mariann	Angel of Efficiency
Nancy	Angel of Productivity
Raymond	Angel of Technology
Sally	Angel of Perseverance

CASE STUDY - *Visualizing the Outcome*
Facing many challenges over the past few years, Kevin triumphed over all of them. As an executive climbing the corporate ladder, he finally found his niche.

After leaving an unhappy relationship and my position at a telecommunications corporation in New York, I returned home to Chicago. Aware that I was busy evaluating career options, a concerned friend suggested we attend an Angel presentation at our local bookstore. That day changed my life forever!

Learning about Angel First Aid Techniques really piqued my interest. Two of the remedies that I found most helpful were "Climb to Success" and "Go for the Gold." Using "Power Surge" strengthened my resolve to succeed. This spiritual drive gave me the confidence needed to secure an executive position with an international corporation.

Once employed, I devised a perfect method for organizing my thoughts, fitting each piece together as if in a puzzle. This allowed me to visualize the preferred outcome and concentrate on rapid results. The system worked well and I received several promotions that tripled my income within the first year. During the initial four months, the company leaders began tapping me for advice. On a personal level, I started dating a woman who shares my belief in Angels.

Kevin's Steps to Success
Look at life as a puzzle—a strategy emerges as you put the pieces together. Make a new plan, then expect a miracle. Rely on mentors, Angels included, to act as sources of wisdom.

REMEDIES

Piece by Piece
Daily responsibilities present obstacles. Reducing tasks to a more workable size will make them much easier to manage. With Jason, Angel of Organization, close by, draw a circle representing the outline of a pie and divide it into six slices. Label the wedges with the concerns you are facing. Note the one requiring the most attention. List actions needed to address or resolve this situation. Then, immediately move on to the next slice. After prioritizing all your responsibilities, ask Jason to help you complete one portion at a time. Take the opportunity to savor every "bite" as you enjoy the sweet taste of accomplishment.

Dosage: Regularly

Yes or No
When initiating a job search, it is imperative to make solid decisions. To determine the career that will best incorporate your life's purpose, use this exercise. Envision Angels standing by; then place your fingertips in the center of the breastbone. Next, choose an occupation and make a short and simple statement to discover if your selection is the most suitable. For example, think about a job as a computer programmer while you say aloud: *Being a computer programmer is the right job for me.* If you lean forward, the answer is "yes." A backward movement will indicate that there is a better option. The body's innate intelligence provides answers to similar questions in other areas of your life. Angels recommend practicing Yes or No as a guidance tool for accurate decision-making.

Dosage: As required

Time Prosperity

Meeting a deadline and organizing a major assignment can be better handled by the use of efficient time management. Taking advantage of "Angelic time" allows you to reach a higher level of productivity. Imagine your chest expanding approximately eight inches on each side. Visualize your upper body remaining in this state, filled with the extra space. The increased capacity produces additional time to perform an extraordinary task quickly and with ease. When you have finished the job, permit your chest to return to its original size.

Dosage: As needed

Follow Through

Determination and commitment are necessary to follow a venture through to fruition. As you tackle a new project, let Nancy, Angel of Productivity, and Sally, Angel of Perseverance, serve as mentors. They are enthusiastic and eager to be of help, so consult with them several times a day. Ask for guidance or advice relevant to a successful completion of your undertaking. Listen intently for the wisdom in their answers. When you begin to understand these messages, additional benefits will become evident. The result is a heightened sense of achievement strengthened by the connection to multiple Angelic sources.

Dosage: When desired

Goal a Day

Efficiency is improved when all your thoughts are in order. The value of this technique is to learn how to write affirmations that will prepare you for ultimate success. With supervision from Mariann, Angel of Efficiency, take a plain sheet of paper and write a goal for the day. Begin the affirmation with *I am*... or *I have*..., making sure that it is uplifting. Select a target date, the exact dollar amount expected, and everything else that is required for attaining the desired outcome. When a task is accomplished, the possibility of reaching small goals increases, thereby developing confidence to pursue and achieve larger ones.

Dosage: Daily

PREVENTATIVE MEDICINE

- ✓ Two remedies, three times a week
- ✓ Three affirmations, two times a week

SUCCESS QUESTIONS

Does Angelic intervention ease responsibility?
Serving as constant companions, Angels will offer the basic tools to make responsibilities much more manageable. The Messengers facilitate organization and provide the means to carry out all duties and tasks. Celestial Beings act as a support system for finishing a project in a viable fashion.

Angel Specialist: Courtney, Angel of Responsibility

Primary Remedy: *Piece by Piece*, page 35

How do Angels initiate productivity?
Angels have unlimited resources available for helping individuals to become more proficient at increasing output. They also create an atmosphere conducive to the completion of assignments with ease. Celestial Beings contribute many ideas and inspire people to maintain focus on current activities.

Angel Specialist: Nancy, Angel of Productivity
Primary Remedy: *Follow Through*, page 36

SECOND OPINION

Rita Emmett — *Public speaker, seminar facilitator, teacher, and consultant to numerous businesses. Author:* The Procrastinator's Handbook: Mastering the Art of Doing It Now.

One real secret to organization and time management is that busy people really do have a choice; they can say "no." When deciding whether to undertake a task, weigh the importance of the request. Prioritizing should take into account that large or costly decisions require much more thought and energy. Be sure to factor in extra time and the genuine possibility of needing additional funds. Each day, write down all your own objectives, commit to them, and you will prosper. Keep in mind that humor combined with enthusiasm is what it takes to sustain a successful lifestyle.

Keywords: Choices. Priorities. Humor.

Miracle Story

Snow Angel

Eleanor, a retired schoolteacher, was visiting relatives in southern Illinois. She made the trip to attend a class reunion nearby. Out of nowhere, Eleanor heard a strong voice urging her to return home.

———————— ✺ ————————

My family was worried and didn't want me to go. They all knew that driving through near-blizzard conditions could be very hazardous; however, a sense of urgency compelled me to depart immediately. While traveling down a quiet, deserted road, I noticed a snow-covered vehicle parked on the shoulder. Several miles later, a familiar, distinctive voice said, "Turn around and go back." It seemed really clear to me that this important directive referred to the car that I had passed.

Ignoring my usually cautious nature, I followed these instructions and quickly headed back to the parked car. By then, it had been covered with two more inches of snow. Brushing off the snowy car revealed a man and a woman huddled around a baby trying to keep the child warm. Surprised, but very relieved to see me, the man, a basketball coach, said that he and his wife and infant son had been stranded for hours.

After driving the very grateful family home, I returned to spend more time with my relatives and shared this incredible story. It is my belief that Archangel Michael was the source of guidance received that eventful day.

———————— ✺ ————————

AFFIRMATIONS

I have found balance.

I am calm and serene.

I have a peaceful life.

I am happy and relaxed.

I have recreational time.

RELAXATION

CONSULTATION

A tranquil mind and body make it possible to reach greater heights. With this harmonious state of being, individuals are able to invest themselves more fully in the realization of their own goals and objectives. Discretionary time is essential in maintaining the flow that allows for ongoing success.

—Joanne, Angel of Relaxation

ANGEL SPECIALISTS

	Archangel Raphael
Alicia	Angel of Serenity
Blake	Angel of Comfort
Eileen	Angel of Happiness
Marilyn	Angel of Leisure
Patrick	Angel of Sports
Perrie	Angel of Music
Robert	Angel of Balance
Susan	Angel of Travel
Tyler	Angel of Abundance
William	Angel of Peace

CASE STUDY - Peace and Prosperity

An advocate of mixing hard work with relaxation, Jonathan knows both are equally important. As a results-oriented professional and entrepreneur, he is open to new ideas.

Already the owner of a thriving manufacturing company, I inherited several large farms. The acquisition of these new properties meant additional responsibility and the stress of paying off associated debt. However, operating the farms also brought great satisfaction.

I am a staunch believer in Angels and always call on them; Michael the Archangel is my greatest supporter. Buying a copy of the *Angel First Aid* book and following the various techniques immediately improved my entire life. "Law of Increase" and "Banking Cash" remedies made generating money to pay off the farms much easier.

Early in my career, I began adding short rest periods to my regular daily routine. Taking ten-minute breaks is a highly effective means of restoring energy and gaining a positive perspective. These respites provide perfect opportunities to practice the Angel First Aid Techniques. The exercises don't take much time and they really work! "Expand Your Territory" helps me to stay focused on achieving financial security. I also subscribe to the motto: *It is good to laugh at yourself.* By tossing in humor, life becomes a lot richer.

Jonathan's Steps to Success

Always tell the truth; a man is as good as his word. Doing favors is better than asking for them. Try to learn something new every day. Taking a break for relaxation is vital.

REMEDIES

Break Room
The future you foresee can become a reality. To bring this to fruition, mentally travel to the space in your body that contains your innermost thoughts and feelings. Visualize the area as a break room in which to relax and regroup. How does it look? Picture the décor and contents. Choose a comfortable place to sit down. Invite your favorite Angels to participate. Imagine a prosperous future, creating all aspects in vivid detail. Make sure to include everything that brings great happiness, comfort, and peace. When the scenario is perfected and you are satisfied with it, keep this sensation for at least one minute. Feeling refreshed and revitalized, leave the break room, knowing that your personal sanctuary is always available to revisit at any time.

Dosage: Daily

Serenity Float
A tranquil environment offers the ideal circumstances to gain additional insight. Picture Alicia, Angel of Serenity, lounging comfortably on a raft and floating down a placid river. She beckons you to join her. Notice a raft by the shore, climb aboard, and push off. While floating alongside Alicia, request her guidance. Phrase the question in this manner: "What do I need to know that I don't already know about _____?" (Insert the subject of your query.) Her response is direct and informative. Utilizing the same formula, continue to ask as many questions as you desire. Once the answers have been obtained, bid the Angel goodbye and begin your return. Upon reaching the shore, take a long walk, reflecting on this newly acquired wisdom and how it will improve your life.

Dosage: As needed

Angelic Choir

Experience the joyful state of relaxation that hearing music engenders. Start by imagining an Angelic Choir singing sweetly in the background. Listen to beautiful, melodious strains that fill the entire surrounding area. Revel in the peacefulness imparted by this music. The song features lyrics so inspiring that they will calm and soothe your soul. Understanding the true meaning of these words, replay all the expressions of comfort for at least one minute. As the singers fade into the distance, you will begin to resonate with their Angelic harmony.

Dosage: Three times a week

Easy Money

Boost the potential to attract and stockpile resources. This exercise helps you to accumulate funds and substantially increase profits. Envision yourself sitting at an executive desk. Tyler, Angel of Abundance, enters the room carrying moneybags overflowing with cash and piles them on the desk. You pick up some currency and feel its texture. Continue touching the money, as you remind yourself how simple it can be to bring all of this abundant wealth into your world. Then, include the practice in your regular routine. Tyler winks and exclaims, "I will return later with more bags filled with cash!" Relax; easy money is on its way.

Dosage: When desired

Coffee Break

Tranquility is vital for a well-balanced lifestyle. Quiet your mind by taking a fifteen-minute coffee break with William, Angel of Peace. Leaving the office together, bring some refreshments and walk along a winding forest path, chatting amicably. William soon inquires, "If inner peace was your top priority, how would you live your life?" Take some time to reflect on this profound question and formulate an answer. When satisfied, communicate your response to the Angel. Solicit his direction in designing and implementing a plan that integrates the enlightening ideas. Enjoying this renewed state allows you to move forward. Return to work assured that you have embarked upon the pathway to peace.

Dosage: Daily

PREVENTATIVE MEDICINE

- ✓ Three remedies, two times a week
- ✓ Two affirmations, four times a week

SUCCESS QUESTIONS

Do Angels play a role in achieving balance?
Busy professionals who involve Celestial Beings in their lives find it easier to stay in balance. With the Guardian Angels as assistants, these individuals become more calm, centered, and settled. This fresh perspective produces a sense of wholeness that gives family and career equal value.

Angel Specialist: Robert, Angel of Balance

Primary Remedy: *Creative Colors*, page 60

How will Angels foster inner peace?
The Messengers recommend living as well as working in a tranquil environment. All Celestial Beings know that peace of mind and a relaxed body are fundamental ingredients for continued success. Cultivating a relationship with the Angels will bring an increased level of comfort and serenity.

Angel Specialist: William, Angel of Peace
Primary Remedy: *Coffee Break*, page 45

SECOND OPINION

Portia Carmichael — *Owner of Smith-Carmichael Financial, analysis and mediation company. Financial planning teacher in Chicago area. Retired economics instructor at Rutgers University.*

Prosperity is a dynamic in which all aspects of one's life—family, career, finances, and recreation—are properly balanced. Success and fulfillment have always been realized when I was focused on my goals with definite deadlines for their accomplishment. I am able to attain prosperity through integrity, perseverance, tenacity, and time management. Achievements that provide me with a great deal of satisfaction are those that benefit others and are not just for personal gain.

Keywords: Integrity. Tenacity. Satisfaction.

New Arrival

After reading an article about Angel First Aid *in the* Daily Herald, *Janet attended a program sponsored by a women's organization. She related this interesting story that describes her granddaughter Cindy's Angelic encounter.*

_____ ✺ _____

My daughter, Susan, and her husband, Jack, had been trying unsuccessfully to have another child. Susan had experienced several miscarriages and the couple was beginning to find the situation quite hopeless. Jack, a prominent obstetrician, was cognizant of the fact that the odds—from a medical standpoint—were not good.

One evening while tucking his daughter into bed, Jack surprised her with the news that they would be visiting Disney World shortly. Early the next morning, Cindy shared some news of her own: "Last night an Angel sat on the end of my bed and told me that my baby brother is going with us. He will be born at Christmas."

Jack was very doubtful, assuming that she was simply remembering a dream. However, the Angelic promise proved to be a fact. Susan was three months pregnant when the family visited Disney World, and baby Jacob was born just one day after Christmas. As for Cindy's conversations with Angels, Jack says, "I'll never doubt her again!"

_____ ✺ _____

AFFIRMATIONS

I am creating abundance.

I have genuine strength.

I am thinking positively.

I have powerful resolve.

I am determined to win.

STRENGTH

CONSULTATION

*P*ersonal power is a fundamental and necessary component of achieving true prosperity. With this increased capacity, individuals have the drive to put their ideas into action and create a secure future. Self-assurance and commitment establish a sturdy foundation upon which to build success.

—Barry, Angel of Strength

ANGEL SPECIALISTS

	Archangel Michael
Caroline	Angel of Positive Thinking
Cory	Angel of Career Development
Deborah	Angel of Interviewing
Esther	Angel of Vitality
Evelyn	Angel of Manifesting
Gunther	Angel of Fitness
Patrick	Angel of Sports
Peter	Angel of Health
Solomon	Angel of Security
Theresa	Angel of Empowerment

CASE STUDY - Following a Positive Example

Diana credits her father with helping her to become a successful person. Paralyzed from the waist down after an accident, Edward inspired others with his bravery and many words of wisdom.

As a customer service representative for one of the nation's largest office supply companies, I rank top in the field by adhering to my father's advice, "Diana, count on yourself."

Owner of a commercial construction business, Dad would welcome all his employees into our home for any reason, maintaining an "open-door policy." As a child, I learned to get along with adults and accept everyone. Seeing how his upbeat attitude served to motivate and strengthen all those around him created a lasting impression on me. Growing up with a disabled parent that always maintained a positive outlook demonstrated quite clearly to me that people can lead productive lives despite adversity.

Reading *Angel First Aid* validates my personal thoughts and feelings. I practice "Goal Setting" and "Backbone" to complement the teachings learned during childhood: that hope, miracles, and the ability to cope are all gifts from the Angels. Having a special connection with Caroline, Angel of Positive Thinking, provides constant reassurance and a sense of mastery over my life. Support from the Celestial Beings, in conjunction with my father's decision to remain optimistic, has encouraged me to follow in his footsteps.

Diana's Steps to Success

Dad's philosophy was to capitalize on all strong points. He always said, "Diana, use your *gift of gab* and let others *hear your smile*." This concept works well in customer service.

50

REMEDIES

Backbone

Great material wealth and rewarding experiences come to individuals who command respect. Practicing this exercise helps to establish boundaries and set limits. It can easily be applied to a situation where courage and resolve are mandated. While setting guidelines or addressing the particular issues, concentrate on your backbone. Request that Theresa, Angel of Empowerment, infuse you with energy. Think about this energy moving from the front to the back of your body and settling in your spine. Notice the extra stamina and improvement in your posture. Each time the remedy is completed, the additional strength allows you to remain steadfast during negotiations and resolute in your convictions.

Dosage: When required

Power Surge

Increasing personal drive supplies the momentum needed to attract new opportunities. Reinforce your performance reserves by accepting a special gift from Archangel Michael. Envision him approaching you carrying an ornate silver breastplate. He places this "Armor of Power" on your chest and fortifies it with energy emitted from the palm of his hand. Feel renewed strength coursing through your body as a result of the mighty power surge. Hold that dynamic sensation for at least one minute. Then, continue to wear the imaginary breastplate with great pride for the entire day; in the evening, hand it back to the Archangel for use at a later date. This technique produces a cumulative effect, making you stronger with each successive repetition.

Dosage: Regularly

Law of Increase

Expanding the scope of an enterprise broadens its financial base. With these simple steps, you can quickly "grow the business" and advance its profitability. Imagine speaking before a group of associates and prospective clients. Your presentation targets a plan to attract wealth and further success. Invite the audience to join in and repeat this phrase: *I invoke the Law of Increase!* Add any other positive statements desired. Visualize Guardian Angels furnishing the funds to expedite your prosperity. Walk away from the podium confident that you have just initiated an opportunity for promoting economic growth.

Dosage: Repeat affirmation every day

Bank Rolls

Develop a comfortable connection with plentiful amounts of money. This creates the accumulation of revenue. Fortify your fiscal position by adding to your portfolio. To begin, take five one-dollar bills, roll in a bundle, and securely fasten with a rubber band. Make several bundles to put anywhere they will be seen regularly: home, office, or car. Place them in your purse or pockets for greater benefit. Evelyn, Angel of Manifesting, nods as she signals you to expect a windfall each time a "stash" is noticed or touched. When discovering currency in familiar places is a daily occurrence, you will acquire substantial wealth.

Dosage: As often as you wish

Go for the Gold

Acting like a winner will allow you to be more successful. This technique is designed to provide the incentive to make strides in that direction. Picture walking toward the center of the stage in an auditorium. All of the Archangels and hundreds of guests have gathered to give you encouragement. Feel victorious as one of the Archangels places a wide ribbon holding a gold medal around your neck. Turn toward the audience to enjoy thunderous applause and a standing ovation. Leaving the stage, make sure to wave and smile at everyone offering congratulations. You are a winner—keep up the good work!

Dosage: When needed, or before an interview

PREVENTATIVE MEDICINE

✓ Four remedies, three times a week
✓ Two affirmations, two times a week

SUCCESS QUESTIONS

Can Angels improve the interviewing process?
Angels are adept at steering applicants in search of employment to vocations that match their unique skills. At interviews, Celestial Beings are always present to render guidance, bolster confidence, and open the channels of communication. They inspire candidates to obtain lucrative positions.

Angel Specialist: Deborah, Angel of Interviewing

Primary Remedy: *Go for the Gold*, page 53

How do Angels further a person's career?
Celestial Beings support anyone who is interested in establishing a profession. They specialize in contributing advice that catalyzes sound decision-making. This beneficial input generates positive results. Collaborating with the Angels ensures that an individual's efforts will be appreciated and rewarded.

Angel Specialist: Cory, Angel of Career Development
Primary Remedy: *Career Bliss*, page 68

SECOND OPINION

Eric Soderholm —*Founder: SoderWorld Holistic Health Center also Front Row Ticket Service. Former third baseman for Chicago White Sox and New York Yankees.*

Throughout my life, the principles that have helped me to succeed are the same ones offered in my seminars. I suggest all participants observe the following guidelines:

> ➤ Learn to love and accept yourself.
> ➤ Always stay in the present moment.
> ➤ Intentions from the heart are your truth.
> ➤ Listen to your body's wisdom (intuition).
> ➤ Your weakest part is your greatest teacher.
> ➤ Know that you are an eternal, spiritual being.

Keywords: Peace. Wisdom. Intuition.

Archangel Rescue

Elizabeth read an interview about Angel First Aid *in the* Chicago Tribune *and scheduled an Angel Party for friends. Linda, a guest, mesmerized everyone with a vivid recollection of an unforgettable childhood experience.*

———————— ◌ ————————

My position as an investment banker probably began when I was eight years old, playing Monopoly® with both my brothers. One evening while we were sitting on the floor engrossed in our game, two men carrying weapons broke into the house.

Even though she was in one of the upstairs bedrooms, Mom heard us screaming. Grabbing a baseball bat, she summoned Archangel Michael and ran quickly down the steps. To our surprise, the brazen intruders bolted out the back door.

I recall turning around and seeing an enormous Angel standing right behind my mother. He was dressed as a warrior and radiated strength. That must have been the reason why the men fled; obviously, they had also seen the powerful Archangel Michael.

Mom was wise to call on the Angel. It is reassuring to know that he can be available to guard and protect my whole family.

———————— ◌ ————————

AFFIRMATIONS

I am whole and complete.

I have happiness every day.

I am sensitive and intuitive.

I have found enlightenment.

I am truly appreciating life.

UNDERSTANDING

CONSULTATION

*G*enuine prosperity is achieved through following the path that leads to a more meaningful way of living. This greater spiritual knowledge evolves from insight and awareness. Contentment ultimately comes from the search for enlightenment and the realization of one's divine purpose.

—Valerie, Angel of Understanding

ANGEL SPECIALISTS

	Archangel Uriel
	Archangel Uriel
Blake	Angel of Comfort
Christopher	Angel of Opportunity
Eileen	Angel of Happiness
Florence	Angel of Compassion
Jonathan	Angel of Business
Nicole	Angel of Negotiation
Robert	Angel of Balance
Sarah	Angel of Harmony
Timothy	Angel of Good Fortune
Ursula	Angel of Alignment

CASE STUDY - Keeping Spiritually in Touch

Sandra became acquainted with Angels in childhood, first feeling their comforting presence while enrolled in nursery school. This celestial guidance eventually led her to the perfect career.

Angels have never left my side. I feel secure knowing they are always nearby. Interacting with them on a regular basis gives me the wherewithal to develop my own personal and entrepreneurial skills. As a "fix-it" child, I was fascinated by human behavior which made the subject of psychology a natural career choice.

The spiritual component of my work furnishes me with a higher level of understanding. Since counseling people is such a great responsibility, I use Angelic communication as an additional resource. Imagine how exciting it was to discover Angel First Aid Techniques, especially "Voice Mail" and "Serenity Float." All the exercises remind me of cookbook recipes, so I follow them to the letter.

Performing these remedies increased my capability to help others. After experiencing the beneficial results of using the book first-hand, I ordered more copies for my practice. *Angel First Aid* supplies us with tools that really support personal growth. It is extremely gratifying to see clients' faces light up when they realize the pieces of their lives can be put back together quite easily.

Sandra's Steps to Success

Hold on to your dream! Never give up or let others dissuade you from doing what seems to be right. Seek out and listen to insightful recommendations from Angels to make decisions.

REMEDIES

Bridge to Success

Happiness is paramount when pursuing a satisfying career. Employ this technique to approach life in a positive manner. Invite Eileen, Angel of Happiness, to stroll with you along a trail to an old wooden bridge. Near the center of this bridge the Angel hugs you gently saying, "Toss all your disappointments, worries, and fears into the river." Using actual arm motions will make the process more effective. Smile as you watch your former blocks to success float away. When these barriers have been released, ask Eileen to surround you with a lavender light. By drawing this spiritual light into your entire body you will feel an incredible sense of joy, hope, and optimism.

Dosage: As necessary

Voice Mail

Successful executives seek sage advice from other people to become top performers. Fortunately, Angelic guidance is just a quick phone call away. Leave a voice mail for Jonathan, Angel of Business. Imagine dialing his number and listening to his greeting that has soft harp music playing in the background. After the beep, explain the situation or circumstance for which you would like to obtain greater insight. Sit quietly and wait for a response. If a reply does not come immediately, your call will be returned as soon as the Angel checks his messages. Requests left on Jonathan's voice mail just before retiring are often addressed by noon the next day. Rest assured, he will get back to you.

Dosage: Four times a week

Negotiating Angels

Effective communication can generate exceptional results. If closing a sale or finalizing a major contract, you can practice this technique. Invite Nicole, Angel of Negotiation, to attend. Picture all the participants wearing navy blue suits. Everyone is extremely interested and listens intently as you give your presentation. Focus on the pertinent issues while utilizing your persuasive skills. Feel exhilarated when negotiations are all favorably completed. Hearty handshakes will signal your success. Leave the meeting, knowing that collaboration with this very knowledgeable Angel Specialist produces mutually beneficial transactions.

Dosage: When required

Creative Colors

The hallmark of a balanced individual is the alignment of mind, body, and spirit. Perform this remedy in order to experience an overall sense of wholeness. See yourself holding all four bricks, one each of these healing colors: pink (physical well-being), sky blue (emotional stability), yellow (mental clarity), and lavender (spiritual development). Visualize the Goddess of Justice holding an old-fashioned scale. As Ursula, Angel of Alignment, observes, place the pink and blue bricks on one side of the scale, the yellow and lavender bricks on the other. Take a deep breath and watch as the scale quickly balances. Welcoming color into your life allows for substantial peace and harmony.

Dosage: As necessary

60

Banking Cash

Understanding the role that money plays in achieving your life's purpose will help to attract the necessary funds. This exercise prepares you for the manifestation of wealth. Envision Timothy, Angel of Good Fortune, giving you a handful of money—all $50 and $100 bills. Every time your hand is extended, Timothy quickly replenishes the generous supply. The Angel also presents several moneybags in which to stuff the cash. When the bags are full, he calls for an armored truck and instructs the driver to deliver these riches to the bank. Rejoice as the plentiful bounty is deposited into your special account where it will multiply into a fortune.

Dosage: Daily, for cash flow

PREVENTATIVE MEDICINE

- ✓ Two remedies, three times a week
- ✓ Three affirmations, two times a week

SUCCESS QUESTIONS

Can Angels foster greater opportunities?

Through celestial assistance many doors can be opened to increase prospects. Guardians inspire people to be successful by cultivating valuable partnerships with experienced mentors. They effectively steer professionals toward appropriate contacts that will broaden business horizons and encourage growth.

Angel Specialist: Christopher, Angel of Opportunity

Primary Remedy: *Expand Your Territory*, page 100

Will Angels aid in attaining happiness?
Celestial Beings know that happiness comes from being centered or feeling complete. Guardian Angels enthusiastically support and facilitate the achievement of this perfect state. A person receives comfort as The Messengers perpetually deliver the blessings that bring peace and contentment.

Angel Specialist: Eileen, Angel of Happiness
Primary Remedy: *Bridge to Success*, page 59

SECOND OPINION

Jeffrey Herman — *Author:* The Insider's Guide to Book Editors, Publishers and Literary Agents (*12 editions*) *and* Write the Perfect Book Proposal. *Agent for more than 450 published books.*

Prosperity is a natural state of existence that is meant for everyone. To attain this kind of enrichment, people must know themselves well enough to be really honest about what drives them. Balanced individuals—those closely in touch with their own intuition—will become successful human beings. People profit from connecting with their spirituality and understanding what it means. Watching my dogs has taught me a lot about living. They don't have big egos, don't question things, yet seem very much in touch with God.

Keywords: Honesty. Spirituality. Balance.

Voice from Above

A producer for an Ohio radio station approached me after learning that Angels were sighted at the scene of an auto accident. During the ensuing program, a listener named Barbara called in to relate a similar situation.

My husband, Jake, invited our three children and me along on a business trip. Rushing to get underway, we didn't remember to buckle up. As we headed down the road, I heard a loud voice warn, *Put on your seat belts!* Quickly checking the children's safety harnesses and fastening my belt, I urged Jake to do the same. But he wasn't fast enough. Just a few moments later, a red car crossed the median, hitting us head-on.

I waited while paramedics worked to save Jake's life. A young man with sandy brown hair sat down beside me. Gently taking my hand, he repeated, "Everything is going to be all right." This caring stranger rode with me in the ambulance and stayed at the hospital. When I inquired about the man's identity, all the nurses were perplexed, stating they had not seen anyone fitting that exact description.

After some thought, it became clear that he must have been my Guardian Angel. I will always be thankful for his comfort and support.

AFFIRMATIONS

I have new, exciting ideas.

I am artistic and creative.

I have exceptional abilities.

I am using my special gifts.

I have many inborn talents.

CREATIVITY

CONSULTATION

$\mathcal{T}$he true essence of creativity is the distinctive expression of innovative ideas. Combining a person's unique talents with inspiration and insight enhances the potential for real success. Frequent utilization of creative and artistic abilities in all areas of one's life furthers personal development.

—Bettina, Angel of Creativity

ANGEL SPECIALISTS

	Archangel Gabriel
Alexander	Angel of Invention
Barbara	Angel of Fame
Blake	Angel of Comfort
Christopher	Angel of Opportunity
Cory	Angel of Career Development
David	Angel of Camaraderie
Jacob	Angel of Education
Perrie	Angel of Music
Rachel	Angel of Inspiration
Rita	Angel of Writing

CASE STUDY - Tapping the Imagination

While searching for a new position, Martha increased her chances by augmenting her natural talents. Imaginative thinking combined with corporate expertise produced a highly marketable executive.

Due to downsizing, I was out of work for nearly two years and it was very difficult not to get discouraged. Each time a prospect fell through, my hopes were shattered again. The Angels became a constant support system and never let me lose faith.

Luckily, I already knew about Angel First Aid Techniques when I needed them the most. During my unemployment, "Confidence Builder" and "Career Bliss," plus "Picture of Success" helped me to reinforce positive thinking. These remedies offered a good way to visualize and manifest the special opportunity that I was seeking. While working for temp agencies, my free time was spent exploring the arts. I filled many hours visiting galleries and taking classes to bolster my creativity.

Everything changed for me when a headhunter located the management position in marketing that turned out to be a perfect match. Overnight my income soared to six figures, literally doubling my previous salary. Now, as a successful executive, I am incorporating artistic perspectives into the world of business. Believing in the Angels has been a great career asset.

Martha's Steps to Success

Always be open to new possibilities. Never give up hope or faith in your ability to succeed. Absolute miracles come from persistently striving to fulfill your various goals.

REMEDIES

Picture of Success
Visualizing prosperity accelerates financial security. Enlist Angelic assistance in raising the bottom line. Imagine an animated painting that represents a thriving business—telephones ringing, employees making appointments, and any other activities that will generate income. Focus on this uplifting scenario for one minute. To maximize profits, capture all the Angels' attention by mentally enlarging your masterpiece until it completely fills the room. This new work of art signals the Celestial Beings to manifest the desired image into reality.

Dosage: Regularly

Morale Booster
When their own input is valued, people are more amenable to making contributions toward a common goal. This vital remedy will improve morale and encourage teamwork. Envision yourself as the coordinator of an important company picnic. The event is significant because it connects or brings together members of the organization nationwide. Management anticipates results. Solicit the assistance of David, Angel of Camaraderie, to help you create an atmosphere that everyone will enjoy. Invite all the employees to brainstorm and encourage them to furnish ideas. See the plan come together accompanied by merriment and laughter. The executive committee, pleased with your results, gives a stamp of approval to move forward with the festivities. David applauds your ingenious strategy devised to promote team performance.

Dosage: Three times a week

Angelic Solution

Making changes occurs easily when there is willingness to adopt a new perspective. Begin this technique by noticing Blake, Angel of Comfort, at your side. Walk together toward a clear, calm pond. Approaching the edge, gather stones and place them in a big pile. Now, look into the water and picture a challenging situation that could be better handled with some additional insight. As an image comes into view, the Angel selects and tosses one of these stones into the pond. She says, "Let all your obstacles disperse in the ripples." Feel the sense of relief that follows. Continue gazing at the surface of the water and watch as an Angelic solution starts to appear. Tell Blake how you intend to incorporate this desirable outcome into your plans for the future.

Dosage: As needed

Career Bliss

Expecting success is the ultimate method of guaranteeing its achievement. Cory, Angel of Career Development, takes you on an exciting adventure. Traveling in a hot air balloon, begin to think about what it would be like to "land" the perfect position. See your new professional environment in detail—include responsibilities, personalities of all colleagues, and management philosophy. The Angel is enthusiastic as he points out your office, its location, and the expansive view from several windows. Exhilaration builds as you envision living this scenario. Preparing to depart, allow Cory to navigate the return trip.

Dosage: Daily, while seeking employment

Dollar Signs

Attract additional funds into your life by using symbols of money. This is a quick and easy remedy for experiencing financial gain. With the index finger of your dominant hand, sketch small dollar signs in the air directly in front of you. Concentrate on these symbols, drawing them larger and larger, until your body becomes involved in the motion. Repeat at least three times, beginning with a small dollar sign. If you have a designated purpose for the money, such as an extended vacation or business development, direct your attention to that goal. Angels respond by supplying greater sums to invest and enjoy.

Dosage: Regularly

PREVENTATIVE MEDICINE

✓ Two remedies, three times a week
✓ One affirmation, two times a week

SUCCESS QUESTIONS

How do Angels increase creativity?

Celestial Beings can help people to cultivate innate gifts as well as enhance artistic talents. They motivate individuals to explore their abilities to reach creative potential. Angels will present innovative ideas and generate opportunities to acquire the skills necessary for attaining success.

Angel Specialist: Bettina, Angel of Creativity

Primary Remedy: *Picture of Success*, page 67

Can Angels boost morale?
Angels will utilize their communicative powers to further positive, uplifting interactions among people. Celestial Beings inspire team efforts and reinforce the value of working together to accomplish goals. The Messengers foster productive, viable associations and promote cooperation.

Angel Specialist: David, Angel of Camaraderie
Primary Remedy: *Morale Booster*, page 67

SECOND OPINION

Peter Lamas — *Leading Hollywood makeup artist and beauty expert: clientele includes Elizabeth Taylor, Cindy Crawford. Film credit:* Titanic. *Founder: Advice website, BeautyWalk.com.*

Happiness indicates a really good relationship with yourself. The optimal way to maintain this state of being is to renew intentions or review goals each day. Never stop learning! Always explore and develop natural talents. Choose your focus, then become highly skilled. Acquire additional knowledge in related areas to enhance versatility. Search out and find experts to study under in the field; that makes all the difference. Consult with Angels as they guide through God's wisdom.

Keywords: Intention. Creativity. Focus.

Irish Broadcast

Shannon, a producer from an Irish radio station, called me to set up an interview. During the actual broadcast, it was obvious that Ryan, the host, was skeptical and even antagonistic. Although people called in to relate their dramatic stories, he remained cynical. Near the end of the show, Archangel Michael told me to notify Ryan to expect a special Angelic encounter in the next forty-eight hours.

Five days later, Shannon called again, saying, "Within the time frame you mentioned on the show, Ryan was mystified by the floral fragrance apparent in his office. He asked several of us to join him to verify the scent, because as far as he knew, there were no flowers at the station. When we gathered together, a beautiful Angel appeared in the corner!"

While listening to Shannon tell her story, I thought to myself, "Archangel Michael kept his promise." In a follow-up conversation, she reported that Ryan was so impressed that he shared this Angelic experience with his audience.

She said, "Your interview and the events that followed caused quite a stir in Ireland."

AFFIRMATIONS

I am positive and optimistic.

I have charm and charisma.

I am in the best profession.

I have great self-confidence.

I am making an impression.

CONFIDENCE

CONSULTATION

Successful, empowered people possess a very strong sense of self-esteem. Unwavering belief in professional capabilities propels those who wish to reach a high level of excellence. Having strength, confidence, and the courage of one's convictions will provide the impetus to advance in life.

—Rebecca, Angel of Confidence

ANGEL SPECIALISTS

	Archangel Gabriel
Barry	Angel of Strength
Caroline	Angel of Positive Thinking
Cornell	Angel of Decision-Making
Deborah	Angel of Interviewing
Jacob	Angel of Education
Katrina	Angel of Prosperity
Melody	Angel of Self-Esteem
Patrick	Angel of Sports
Samuel	Angel of Excellence
Theresa	Angel of Empowerment

CASE STUDY - Developing the Self Within
From a young age, Angela dreamed of becoming a talk show host. Natural self-confidence and diligence have paid off. Currently, her broadcasts reach large audiences with information that promotes spiritual development.

Bonnie, my neighbor, worked at a radio station sponsoring "Take Your Daughter to Work Day." Having no children of her own, she invited me to tag along. Although I was only 10 years old, it was a life-defining experience. From that time on, establishing a career in radio became my ultimate goal. In high school, I was class president and excelled in sports. These activities boosted my confidence and helped me feel comfortable appearing in front of an audience.

Now living my dream, working for a major network, I am able to offer programming that makes a big difference by contributing to others. Interviewing guests with inspiring, uplifting messages is my favorite thing to do. The authors of new self-help books are especially welcome. By having The Angel Lady on my show, I learned about Angel First Aid Techniques.

These remedies have been an incredible blessing. "Morale Booster" and "Energy Tap" make great warm-up exercises before each broadcast. I regularly check in with Archangel Gabriel for any last-minute advice. Radio and Angels will always be a part of my world.

Angela's Steps to Success
Whenever possible, follow your inner guidance. Choose personal growth as a lifelong objective. Start working on a career as soon as possible to gain knowledge and skill.

REMEDIES

The Judge

Releasing self-sabotaging habits is necessary for initiating change. Do you advance just so far, reach a plateau, and then stop progressing? Most likely you are being hampered by disparaging thoughts that originate from a source often called "The Judge." His presence in your life stems from disapproving attitudes or critical remarks received during childhood. To clearly identify The Judge, recognize the warning sign that represents his stronghold: a feeling of having done something wrong. Defuse The Judge's power over you by writing down all his detrimental comments, those messages transmitted through negative self-talk. Shred the paper and throw it away. Now, ready to move on, accept praise and approval from the Angels as they reaffirm your good qualities. List these positive attributes and review them during the day.

Dosage: Often

Academic Excellence

Comprehending information and using it productively are imperative to attaining success. If pursuing academic excellence, ask Jacob, Angel of Education, to guide your quest for knowledge. Imagine your name on the dean's list. Revel in the satisfaction of having earned this scholarly achievement. Go one step further and see yourself graduating with honors. You are empowered by all the expressions of happiness from Jacob, family members, and many friends. Hold that feeling of success for at least one minute. Extend this newfound confidence to other types of activities.

Dosage: As necessary

Wealth Affirmation

Strong feelings of self-worth prepare the way to receiving real abundance. Perform this remedy to attract financial growth. Rebecca, Angel of Confidence, will help to establish a continuous supply of revenue. Think of ways to use the extra income. Tapping gently on each temple, say: *I give myself permission to be wealthy!* Repeat the affirmation with conviction at least five times. Writing this statement during the day is highly beneficial to increasing its effect. Rebecca will be made aware of your intention and carry the declaration to the Angelic Realm for immediate action.

Dosage: Daily, for at least one month

Instant Replay

Visualizing athletic triumphs is the key to making them a reality. Select Patrick, Angel of Sports, to join your team. Practice this technique to prepare for a big game. Envision every step you will take to win. Be meticulous, pinpointing motions or actions to improve your performance. Replay the routine until it is flawless. Then, picture yourself exulting in the thrill of victory! Feel elated and maintain this high level of enthusiasm for at least one minute. When you actively participate in a sport, imagine Patrick cheering from the sideline. As successful achievement of athletic events is realized, transfer this sense of victory to future endeavors.

Dosage: Regularly or on weekends

⌒ **Confidence Builder**
Self-assurance is one of the best ways to make a favorable impression. Using this exercise is especially advantageous prior to a job interview. Deborah, Angel of Interviewing, is standing close by to differentiate your capabilities from those of other candidates. With your hand, rub across the bottom of your rib cage five times (each back-and-forth movement counts as one time). Then, with arms crossed over your chest, grasp the upper arms just below your shoulders. Rub briskly up and down five times. Placing both hands on the outside of your thighs, apply slight pressure, and slide them from hip to knee five times. The interviewer will notice an increase in your energy that makes you appear more confident and capable.

Dosage: As needed

PREVENTATIVE MEDICINE
✓ Two remedies, three times a week
✓ Two affirmations, four times a week

SUCCESS QUESTIONS

Can Angels maximize education?
Having a close connection with Celestial Beings enables students to research as well as integrate relevant material. The Messengers eagerly promote academic pursuits by expanding comprehension and ensuring the retention of information. They encourage timely completion of assignments.

Angel Specialist: Jacob, Angel of Education
Primary Remedy: *Academic Excellence*, page 75

Do Angels help with athletic endeavors?
Increasing physical stamina is one of the Angels' contributions to professional and weekend athletes. Celestial Beings also endorse visualization techniques to motivate sports enthusiasts in search of enhanced performance. Guardian Angels champion those striving for this type of excellence.

Angel Specialist: Patrick, Angel of Sports
Primary Remedy: *Instant Replay*, page 76

SECOND OPINION

Steven Belkin — *Chairman of the Board: Trans National Group. Trustee: Cornell University, Harvard Business School, Hoffman Institute, and Boston Medical Center. Founder: 26 corporations.*

"Conceive it … believe it … achieve it!" This motto has guided me throughout a lengthy and prosperous entrepreneurial career. Most important is "believing it" or believing in your own capabilities. Successful people grow and learn from tough times and celebrate the good times. You must possess a greater sense of purpose than simply making money. In all of my companies, our primary goals include supporting employees' personal growth, offering quality products, and having fun. With this design, profits just flow.

Keywords: Conceive. Believe. Achieve.

Miracle Story

Just in Time

Nearly twelve years ago, Jason's family survived a life-threatening situation. After hearing me on the radio in Washington State, Jason wrote to ask the names of his Angels and included this story.

————————— ✻ —————————

We had a terrible fire at our house when I was 12. My younger brother Ted and I shared a bedroom and were asleep as flames broke out. Although the smoke alarm was broken, Ted woke up just in time and screamed, "Fire!" I shot out of bed, grabbed him, then ran for the nearest window.

In a real panic, I did not even try to open it but instead punched through two panes of glass and a screen with my bare hand. Despite being scraped by many shards of glass as we crawled out the broken window, both of us emerged virtually unharmed. Later, the fire marshal remarked that between the defective smoke alarm and the intensity of the blaze, it was a genuine miracle that my whole family had escaped.

The feelings of courage and immortality I experienced that night still remain strong. Others might say it was an adrenaline rush, but I know that Angels saved my family and me. Today, as a firefighter, I always contact the Angels when the fire bell rings.

————————— ✻ —————————

AFFIRMATIONS

I have vitality and health.

I am incredibly energized.

I have a great zest for life.

I am strong and powerful.

I have the fuel for success.

ENERGY

CONSULTATION

*P*rosperity is accelerated by establishing a balance that effortlessly links all energies—mental, physical, and spiritual. Personal advancement can be fueled by the connection and positive interaction generated by this harmonious trio. Maximizing the flow builds energy for success.

—Paula, Angel of Energy

ANGEL SPECIALISTS

	Archangel Raphael
Barry	Angel of Strength
Esther	Angel of Vitality
Gunther	Angel of Fitness
Katrina	Angel of Prosperity
Mirra	Angel of Healing Arts
Patrick	Angel of Sports
Peter	Angel of Health
Randolph	Angel of Expansion
Robert	Angel of Balance
Ursula	Angel of Alignment

CASE STUDY - *Powering up for Education*

As a talented academic, Priscilla displays her effectiveness in the classroom. Using visualization, this popular university professor faces a rigorous daily routine with boundless energy.

The need to be "on" is imperative because student aptitude advances when lessons are conveyed with vigor. During a seminar, I discovered the benefits of practicing Angel First Aid. Original techniques have been specifically designed for career performance. "Vitality Plus" and "Twisting" are the two best remedies to fortify my stamina and double my teaching ability! Through research on left- and right-brain functions, I found that there was a specific type of music to improve attention span and focus. Based on these findings, I recommend the use of "Baroque Beat."

Being open to accepting alternative sources of knowledge and observing life through other people's eyes assisted me in identifying what was truly important. I have noticed that success increases at the same rate as a person can project or channel energy. So, Barry, Angel of Strength, is my ever-present adjunct in the classroom.

Watching students grow as they broaden their minds and gain confidence is very rewarding. My investment of time and energy pays off when these young scholars reach their full potential.

Priscilla's Steps to Success

Achievement has always meant focusing on a specific goal, setting a deadline, and doing what it takes to meet that objective. For me, *Everything is energy, and energy is everything.*

82

REMEDIES

Energy Tap
Demonstrating exuberance will improve the likelihood of becoming successful. While practicing the following remedy, ask for Angelic blessings and intervention. To start, put one hand over your navel. With the other hand, tap these three areas at least seven times: underneath the collarbones where they are connected to the breastbone, just above the upper lip, and then beneath the lower lip. Switch hands and repeat. This form of rejuvenation returns the flow of energy to its correct pattern. Recharge mental and physical batteries to help invigorate all pursuits.

Dosage: Four times a week

Vitality Plus
Enhancing personal strength dramatically increases your financial stability. This technique improves stamina by balancing metabolism. Place your non-dominant hand on your throat. Drop the other arm to your side, with index finger pointed down. Begin spinning the wrist quickly in a clockwise circle while counting to forty. Esther, Angel of Vitality, playfully counts along with you. After finishing this process, note the immediate difference in your energy level. Adapt this powerful exercise into your routine for tangible results. Vitality Plus is a valuable tool to expedite general and overall well-being.

Dosage: Daily

Twisting

Regular infusions of employee enthusiasm will further any organization's plan for success. With this remedy, you can sharpen mental acuity and also build energy. Start by stretching both arms out to the side, keeping them at shoulder height. Then, twisting at the waist, swing your arms rhythmically from side to side. Focus on prosperous thoughts while performing this exercise to music. Invite a few Angels to join in—they imitate the motion by using their wings. Celestial Beings will not tire, so twist as long as you like. Be prepared for the positive charge that propels you and the company forward.

Dosage: Whenever a boost is needed

Power Coins

Concentrate on fulfilling personal and professional goals. As you picture a beautiful rainbow that consists of vibrant colors, notice Katrina, Angel of Prosperity, approaching. She is carrying a large pot of golden coins and places it at your side. Energized by the bounty, you are now prompted to create more. Contemplate for at least one minute the many ways available to raise capital. Then, thank Katrina for being extremely generous and sharing all of this abundance. Make it your intention to transform the cache of gold into genuine wealth.

Dosage: Often, for monetary growth

Energy Ball

In today's corporate environment, maintaining stamina is crucial for anyone who wishes to excel. Practice this technique to become more dynamic. Imagine that you are forming a snowball as you gather and shape celestial energy into a sphere. When you begin to feel the force between your palms, continue "packing" for another fifteen seconds. Now position the ball at your navel and sense the energy being absorbed into your body. Peter, Angel of Health, watches as you radiate this new strength. Leave the energy ball in place in order to intensify its potent force. The effects of this process are cumulative, significantly enhancing your potential to exhibit personal power.

Dosage: Daily

PREVENTATIVE MEDICINE

✓ Two remedies, two times a week
✓ One affirmation, three times a week

SUCCESS QUESTIONS

What can Angels do to improve health?
A Guardian Angel's mission is to assist individuals in sustaining their mental and physical well-being. The Messengers endorse the adage: *If you have your health, you have your wealth.* They also emphasize a wholesome style of living that elevates performance and invites continuous prosperity.

Angel Specialist: Peter, Angel of Health
Primary Remedy: *Vitality Plus*, page 83

Will Angels assist in raising the bottom line?
Angels share their celestial expertise to produce outstanding fiscal results. They willingly contribute information and inspire ideas for promotion, advertising, and public relations. Always accessible for boosting sales, Celestial Beings help to energize and motivate executives to generate affluence.

Angel Specialist: Randolph, Angel of Expansion
Primary Remedy: *Money Magnet*, page 99

SECOND OPINION

Darla Rowe — *Vice President of Oakmont Mortgage in Northern California, the company's leading branch. Former Vice President: Association of Professional Mortgage Women.*

Whatever my objective is at the time, I always find it advantageous to visualize myself completing it successfully. Another key factor is playing the role by dressing and acting powerfully, even when discouraged. Positive energy attracts positive response. In other words, "Walk the walk, and talk the talk." I expect success and take ownership of it; then the outcome is guaranteed. Most importantly, I count on my faith to help me attain my goals. Successful people have already arrived there in their minds—100 percent.

Keywords: Energy. Visualization. Perseverance.

Angelic Command

Celestial Beings serve as lifelong friends and companions. During a radio program listeners called in and shared Angel stories. This one is profound and involves two generations.

―――――――――― ∽ ――――――――――

My father, at 34, was an influential minister. In the fall of 1979, my parents' car was hit head-on by a drunk driver. Trapped inside the mangled wreck, they were both presumed dead. An Angel who was at the scene knew the truth and shouted to a paramedic, "Jump up and get her out now! She is still alive." (The paramedic later testified to this in court.) While using the Jaws of Life to extricate my mother, the rescue team found a very faint pulse. Mom, 31 at the time of the accident, related that she saw my father surrounded by Angels as he walked up a hill into the light.

Twenty years later, in the fall of the year that I turned 31, I also survived a car crash. At 70 miles an hour, my vehicle spun out of control and flipped over, throwing me from the SUV on the first roll. Amazingly, it felt as if an Angel wrapped me in his powerful arms, pulled me through the driver's window, and placed me on the grass. Despite hitting the ground at high speed, I never lost consciousness and no bones were broken. Angels must have also guided the SUV because it landed only inches from my head!

―――――――――― ∽ ――――――――――

AFFIRMATIONS

I am receiving wealth.

I have financial security.

I am attracting mentors.

I have Angel assistants.

I am accepting support.

SUPPORT

CONSULTATION

*E*veryone, including seasoned professionals, benefits from the guidance and encouragement of others. Staying on the fast track of career development can be accomplished by inviting valuable mentors and colleagues into your life. A reliable support system provides increased financial security.

—Harold, *Angel of Support*

ANGEL SPECIALISTS

	Archangel Michael
Barry	Angel of Strength
Cheryl	Angel of Customer Relations
Christopher	Angel of Opportunity
Jacob	Angel of Education
Jordan	Angel of Teamwork
Kyle	Angel of Partnership
Leslie	Angel of Diplomacy
Loretta	Angel of New Enterprise
Marcus	Angel of Sales
Solomon	Angel of Security

CASE STUDY - *Accepting a Helping Hand*

Annette first heard about social work on TV. However, 20 years passed before she was able to pursue her special dream. As the sole means of support for two young children, Annette was determined to update her professional skills and improve her self-esteem.

Working part-time for a local university made it possible to enroll in several courses. One day, a classmate invited me to attend an *Angel First Aid* seminar which resulted in a lasting relationship with Celestial Beings.

As a single parent, I encountered numerous social barriers. However, my steadfast faith in Angels pulled me through. Assisted by Jacob, Angel of Education, I earned both my bachelor's and master's degrees in social work.

Very grateful for the major improvement higher education had made in my world, I wanted to share this same type of success with others who were in similar situations. The perfect opportunity, heading up a women's development program at my alma mater, became available.

Embracing positive action, we use the "Angel Scrapbook" remedy as the primary tool for success. Students actually enjoy identifying their unique abilities and designing their own individual career paths. In addition, we also practice the "Follow Through" remedy on a daily basis and ask our Angels for their invaluable advice.

Annette's Steps to Success

First and foremost, listen to and follow your own inner guidance. Second, pursue an advanced education. Third, satisfy the desire to be of service. You can always rely on Angelic support.

REMEDIES

Meeting an Angel
Connecting with the right people is integral to building an organization. Employing this exercise will help to make profitable business connections. Playing the part of an entrepreneur who is attending a networking event, you arrive, dynamic and filled with energy. Loretta, Angel of New Enterprise, and Leslie, Angel of Diplomacy, join in for support. They are close by as you greet and shake hands with the other attendees. Each person enthusiastically endorses your intriguing ideas and strategies for success. Continue to "work the room," gaining much more confidence with each new contact. Hold this feeling for one minute. Leaving the group, know that Loretta and Leslie are readily available to initiate constructive, professional relationships.

Dosage: Three times a week

Sales for Success
Effective marketing stimulates financial growth through increased sales. Performing this technique will help to jump-start your own company. Visualize a scenario in which Marcus, Angel of Sales, is a regional manager giving a seminar entitled "Meeting and Exceeding Quotas." The energy level in the room heightens noticeably during his pep talk. He details the procedures necessary to guarantee customer satisfaction, then discusses identifying and reaching target markets. Reflect on these points and how they can be implemented as resources to stimulate product interest. Finally, Marcus highlights benefits that can be accrued through association with the Angelic Realm. After the seminar breaks up, be assured that incorporating these recommendations into your business will result in success.

Dosage: Regularly

Play Money

Generating revenue for recreational activities is desirable. Develop additional prosperity for enjoyment by using this remedy. Carry play money similar to that in the game called "Life" which includes $100,000 bills. The Angels nod approvingly as you place these symbols of affluence in your pocket, wallet, or purse. Also, firmly affix currency to your computer, bulletin board, or car visor; anywhere it can be seen often. Each time the "money" is noticed or touched, imagine possessing the same amount of real cash. Then, repeat this affirmation three times: *I expand my wealth tolerance.* When you become accustomed to having large denominations of cash on hand, greater quantities will enter your life.

Dosage: Daily, for additional funds

Solid Foundation

Teamwork is pivotal to all types of flourishing businesses. Uniting singular efforts toward a common purpose becomes easier with this particular technique. Jordan, Angel of Teamwork, acts as your advisor at a construction site. Imaginary blueprints represent plans for achieving objectives. Together with your crew, develop a strategy that will bring this project to fruition. Delegate all tasks to appropriate people. Pay close attention when they offer innovative ideas and discuss their roles. Enthusiasm builds as the participants feel valued. They know the achievement of their goals will enable the entire company to prosper. Ask Jordan, along with the team, to finalize the plans.

Dosage: Two times a week

Business Honors

Executives as well as employees feel validated by having their efforts rewarded. Focus on the importance of your numerous contributions by practicing the following remedy. In this scenario, you have just won the industry's Customer Service Award. Cheryl, Angel of Customer Relations, requests an interview on behalf of *Professional Business* magazine. She begins, "Please share some tips for success." You reply, "Be a good listener, attend to customer needs, and provide quality service." Cheryl, curious about your people skills, queries, "Is anything else important when interacting with others?" Your response: "Treat everyone the way you would like to be treated." Impressed with the answers, the Angel offers congratulations and presents you with a sizable cash award.

Dosage: As needed

PREVENTATIVE MEDICINE

✓ Two remedies, two times a week
✓ Three affirmations, two times a week

SUCCESS QUESTIONS

Will Angels facilitate team building?

Camaraderie as well as compatibility are paramount to creating a profitable organization. Celestial Beings can enhance partnerships between individuals striving to work together. Mutually beneficial conclusions to assignments will be fostered by an "Angel Team" in the work environment.

Angel Specialist: Jordan, Angel of Teamwork

Primary Remedy: *Solid Foundation*, page 92

Can Angels improve customer relations?

Angels will set the stage for creating a win-win situation. Always present to stimulate lucrative consumer interactions, they ensure a productive outcome for all involved. Celestial Beings accelerate success in the marketplace by focusing their attention on providing quality customer care.

Angel Specialist: Cheryl, Angel of Customer Relations
Primary Remedy: *Business Honors*, page 93

SECOND OPINION

Jennifer White — *President: JWC Group. Author:* Work Less, Make More: Stop Working So Hard & Create The Life You Really Want! *and* Drive Your People Wild Without Driving Them Crazy.

Clarifying and writing down goals is my first step to success. Next, I find ways to express my dreams by telling everyone about the ideas. After others buy into my objectives and adopt them as their own, miracles begin to happen. The last step is releasing my ego. That means listening to my intuition and to the Angels' advice. When tuned in, it is easier to tap into the divine place where I can create what is desired. By paying attention or accepting guidance, everything will work out perfectly. The secret of success is to trust yourself and have faith in that inner voice; however, that is often the hardest part.

Keywords: Clarity. Trust. Communication.

Miracle Story

Protector Angel

At the conclusion of an Angel Party, Betty insisted on scheduling a personal consultation for the next afternoon. During our session, she eagerly shared her vivid encounter with a "Physical Angel."

Driving from Springfield to Chicago, I found myself alone on a deserted highway. Without warning, a man in a pickup truck deliberately tried to force my car off the road.

Although frightened, I knew that Archangel Michael was the great protector so I cried out, "Help me!" As if in answer to the plea, a motorcyclist appeared, his face concealed by a bluish helmet. This "Protector Angel" managed to maneuver his cycle between the vehicles and stayed there the entire time, no matter what speed we were going.

Eventually, the truck driver became so frustrated that he exited the interstate. However, several miles down the road, the same pickup reappeared, heading straight toward me. Once again my protector intervened on my behalf. After another fifteen miles of harassment, the aggressor gave up and left the highway. I'm extremely grateful the Archangel was on alert and kept me safe.

AFFIRMATIONS

I am a successful person.

I have an affluent lifestyle.

I am genuinely appreciated.

I have an abundant income.

I am known for my talents.

SUCCESS

CONSULTATION

*T*he true measure of success is the degree to which people experience contentment and fulfillment. As individuals follow a spiritual path, they realize a sense of satisfaction. When enjoying happiness, abundance, and prosperity, everyone can flourish and be fortunate in all facets of life.

—George, Angel of Success

ANGEL SPECIALISTS

	Archangel Michael
Christopher	Angel of Opportunity
Eileen	Angel of Happiness
Evelyn	Angel of Manifesting
Jeremiah	Angel of Financial Security
Jonathan	Angel of Business
Katrina	Angel of Prosperity
Loretta	Angel of New Enterprise
Nicole	Angel of Negotiation
Randolph	Angel of Expansion
Samuel	Angel of Excellence

CASE STUDY - Experiencing a Fulfilled Life

As a teenager, Andrew learned from his father the steps it took to be successful as an entrepreneur. Years later, Andrew's sons receive the benefit of his expertise passed down through generations.

Before the age of 20, I had made two significant decisions. First, education must be top priority, not just for personal growth but also to be a better person. In an effort to find the most fulfilling career, I tried everything that interested me, earning law, accounting, and psychology degrees. During college, I invested my time and resources in buying and rehabbing homes.

After exploring various opportunities, my primary focus became property development. As the owner of multiple shopping centers and housing complexes, I have attained many long-standing goals and shared the rewards of my success with others. The advice I give my sons is, "Get a good education and appreciate your blessings."

The second decision was to make "play" a special part of my life. I incorporate this attitude into the children's books that I write as well as into my daily routine. When a friend sent me a copy of *Angel First Aid,* I began conversing with Samuel, Angel of Excellence, and chose "Play Money" as a favorite remedy. My desire has always been to combine achieving prosperity with having fun.

Andrew's Steps to Success
Never stop learning or finding ways to acquire higher education. Pursue the better things in life, still taking time to play. Encourage other people to follow their own paths.

REMEDIES

Climb to Success

For substantial abundance, it is important to remember and appreciate your history of accomplishments, especially those from which you have progressed. Mentally prepare yourself to scale the mountain of success. Wear appropriate gear to make the journey easier. With each step taken, realize that you are a very competent climber and can make it up to the top. Reaching the summit, review your triumphs, acknowledging Angels, consultants, and business associates who provided mentoring along the way. Recognize the benefits garnered from your positive experiences. On descending, express gratitude for the many forms of guidance and support that have been available throughout your lifetime.

Dosage: Three times a week

Money Magnet

A continuous flow of revenue denotes prosperity. Employ this exercise as a valuable tool to increase funds and amass wealth. Jeremiah, Angel of Financial Security, becomes a key player. See him approaching. He sends out a beam that magnetizes your being. You now have the power required to attract prosperity. The Angel suggests repeating this affirmation: *I am a Mighty Money Magnet!* Speak with deliberate enthusiasm as you picture currency winging toward you from every direction. This potent statement combined with Jeremiah's special force completes the whole process. Now, catch the cash that sparks financial growth and independence.

Dosage: Daily, for additional funds

School of Success

Reach goals and realize objectives by using visualization. Underscore the ability to excel through following this technique. It revolves around receiving a degree from the "School of Success." As the class valedictorian, graduating *summa cum laude*, you have been selected to give the commencement speech. Notice everyone proudly watching your presentation. Relate to the guests what you learned about achieving success. Attentively, the audience listens while you focus on the importance of pursuing one's life purpose. The sound of applause fills the air as George, Angel of Success, is shaking your hand and giving you a diploma. When thanking him, consider the potential that having this degree will generate.

Dosage: As needed

Expand Your Territory

Allowing for growth is an obligatory factor in any business strategy. Practice this remedy to create a reliable plan that secures the continuance of a highly profitable and productive enterprise. Ask Randolph, Angel of Expansion, to contribute his expertise for enlarging your territory. Imagine a giant map shaded to designate all the regions currently served by your organization. Selecting the geographical areas you want to cover, highlight these broadened boundaries with a blue marker. Include the extended borders that determine your organization's vision for the future. Establishing new parameters lets the Angels know exactly where their blessings are needed and can be most effective.

Dosage: Regularly

Shower of Money

Angelic encouragement builds the foundation for making progress. Using this technique, imaginatively set in a ticker-tape parade, ensures willingness to accept affluence. Envision yourself being seated on the back of a convertible. The car is surrounded by people cheering and clapping. Interspersed throughout the crowd, the Angels are thrilled and smiling with pride. Bask in the glory of $100 bills showering down from above. As the excitement builds from this ultimate tribute, hold the feeling for one minute. Near the end of the parade route, give a triumphant wave, knowing that you are well prepared to climb the Steps to Success.

Dosage: Daily

PREVENTATIVE MEDICINE

✓ Two remedies, three times a week
✓ Two affirmations, two times a week

SUCCESS QUESTIONS

Do Angels accelerate victory?
Celestial Beings motivate professionals to perfect their visions of excellence. As consultants, The Messengers assist individuals in attaining much higher levels of performance and realizing dreams. These Guardians offer their charges great possibilities for making connections with business allies.

Angel Specialist: George, Angel of Success

Primary Remedy: *Shower of Money*, page 101

Can Angels impact financial security?
Guardian Angels make sure that their protégés have the necessary capital to fund ventures. Working together in the Angelic Realm, Celestial Beings furnish resources to fulfill monetary aspirations. They encourage the development of inherent gifts that will aid in promoting prosperous growth.

Angel Specialist: Jeremiah, Angel of Financial Security
Primary Remedy: *Law of Increase*, page 52

SECOND OPINION

Kyle Koch — *Founder: Oz Management Consulting, Inc. Former director of recruiting for Kanbay, Inc. Past member: Technology Advisory Board for Loyola and DePaul Universities.*

Success is something that can be achieved through action fueled by human energy. While most people just wait and hope for it to happen, plans should always be made to obtain it. In addressing my objectives, I search for opportunities to learn new skills. This means exploring other fields of interest and capitalizing on my talents. The formula that has helped me gain success is to analyze the situation, devise a strategy, and then implement the plan. I also make it a goal to look for individuals who can provide guidance and mentoring. Remember that it is people—not companies—that further your career.

Keywords: Analyze. Plan. Implement.

Executive Assistant

Paul, CEO of an international corporation, refers to his Guardian Angel in an unusual way. In this story he reveals the extraordinary miracles that his specific Angel delivered.

During my youth, a little on the wild side, I survived intact thanks to my Executive Angel. Years later, our son Jeremy was born with the umbilical cord wrapped twice around his neck. Watching the intense drama of doctors trying to keep him alive, my knees buckled. I pleaded with my Angel to save our son. He did; today Jeremy is a healthy five-year-old.

When friends had their first child, a premature baby, my urgent request was for a special Junior Angel to be temporarily assigned to me while my Executive Angel helped their newborn. In church the following day, I considered asking my Angel's name and wondered if I would trust the answer.

Just an hour later, I picked up the newspaper from my driveway and saw The Angel Lady. The feature article mentioned that she would give people the names of their Angels. I was in tears! How often does an answer come so darn clearly? The only way this could have been more obvious is if a sign posted on the front lawn read, "Your Guardian Angel's name is ____."

—— *Prescription* ——

"*Man's mind, once strengthened by a new idea, never regains its original dimensions.*"

---*Oliver Wendell Holmes*

Prescription for Success

*A*special knowing, feeling, or satisfaction comes from being attuned to spiritual guidance. The professionals who share the following experiences have made this connection. Although success means something different to each of these individuals, trusting their own abilities and acting on their inner wisdom have—in every case—made life more worthwhile.

Jill St. John — *Morning producer/co-host: Y-94FM, Clear Channel - Fargo.*

I have gained prosperity by making career decisions that are based on what I *feel* in my heart and soul, rather than on what I *think*. This philosophy has never failed me and is a result of living with faith. The more you rely on faith, the more evidence appears to show that you are not alone. What peace this brings!

Another important factor has been my strength when handling big disappointments. If you are meant to have something, it's yours. Be patient; it may take time.

Finally, laugh everyday and never take life too seriously. Angels teach us to be joyful and to play. These are all the things that have helped me—and of course, it doesn't hurt that Katrina, Angel of Prosperity, is my Guardian Angel.

Anita Belkin — *Retired. Leading salesperson: Jacobsons, East Grand Rapids, Michigan.*

You cannot go forward if you are looking back.

Tom Fuller — *Singer/songwriter. CEO: Fullco Industries, industrial product distribution company.*

It is God's will for us to be successful. In my creative role, there is no question that songs are "sent" to me. A healing process results from writing about human struggles and emotions. People identify with the feelings behind my music.

For business, ask to be shown a specific endeavor in which you can succeed. Take the first step—that's critical—you really have to try. Continue to use baby steps that will, in time, amount to giant leaps. Perseverance is the foundation for success. Absolutely never give up under any circumstances. Always go the extra mile—winners do what losers don't want to do.

———————————

Karon Gibson — *Author:* Nurses on Our Own. *Host of two TV shows. On-location nurse to film stars.*

When I was young and asked for something, my father would say "no." Then, it was my job to convince him to change his answer to "yes." Because of that, whenever anyone in business told me "no," I just figured I would change that person's mind.

The Angels have played an important role in my life, consistently guiding me. When I didn't want to leave a job, but was forced to move on, it turned out to be in my best interest.

Never underestimate the value of encouragement from someone. My husband has helped me to believe in my abilities. While other people laughed at my dream of writing a book, he knew the truth. It was his belief in me, as well as my drive, that made it all possible.

Raz Ingrasci — *President: Hoffman Institute. Thirty-year veteran of the healing potential movement.*

To be successful, people need to follow their own heart as well as use their mind. If your heart is not on the right path, you cannot be happy. We heal when we contribute to the world, so attend to your own healing. Finding wholeness is truly essential and necessitates changes in one's behavior plus the emergence of spiritual values. I know that this makes a person's path more apparent. Support, care, and guidance will be made available on the journey.

Deborah Benton — *Author:* Lions Don't Need to Roar *and coordinator/presenter of leadership seminars.*

My father is the role model in my life. From him I learned the value of using wisdom as a success tool. Now a consultant, I endorse this philosophy: 1) sometimes things happen in business and life that are unpredictable, but you must stay the course; 2) work hard early on and do not waste any time, not even an hour or a day; 3) keep at it: often one attempt, one phone call, or one letter is not enough; 4) get better as you keep at it, each time improving yourself and the approach; 5) perform your activities fearlessly—move forward by accomplishing what you did not even think that you could do; and 6) present a happy, successful persona. Your character, motivation, and goodness will determine the kind of human being you are.

Elizabeth Larkam — *Pilates expert. Trainer: Cirque du Soleil. Former dance instructor, Stanford University.*

When I have the opportunity to be in divine flow within myself and to facilitate that experience for other people, I am deeply satisfied. For me, this is the feeling of real success. A prayer that I say many times during the day offers guidance in that direction: *Transform me to be in harmony with the flow of divine love, in divine time, and for the highest good of all concerned.* These are the elements that point me toward success. I am blessed with very wise mentors and recommend seeking out enlightenment from these extraordinary types of individuals.

Daphne, my younger sister, was born with a number of handicaps and is unable to speak. However, she has a phenomenal sensitivity to music. When we were children, my singing and dancing soothed or comforted her. That's how we communicated. Now, it is my task to be out in the world healing others through music and movement, with Daphne as my silent partner.

Joe Gentile — *Philanthropist. Owner: Chrysler dealership. Founder: WJJG radio station.*

Entering a career in sales, I wanted to be the number one salesman, and I was. A primary requisite for success is service, taking care of your customers. This involves always being nice to people as well as being competitive in your price. At the dealership and the radio station, our goals are to be honest and aboveboard, believe in the products we sell, and to back up what we say. Also, in all aspects of sales, it is imperative to be a good listener. Taking these facts into consideration, the bottom line still is this: Put in the time and effort needed to be the best. That's success!

Major Belkin — *Founder: Major Machinery Company, East Grand Rapids, Michigan.*

> If you are going to be on the team, be the captain.

Jan Nathan — *Director: Publishers Marketing Association, representing 3,500 book, audio, and video publishers.*

A love of books and a desire to assist people in attaining their goals have been important to me both personally and professionally. My entire family empowered me. I felt that I could achieve anything if I wanted it with my whole being.

The most difficult challenge of my life was when I had to hire and begin to manage people. As an entrepreneur, I did so much myself that allowing others to do projects their own way took time. Today my staff is one of the greatest joys of my career.

If passion for your work plus happiness in your personal life equals success, then I am a very successful person.

Chuck LaFrano — *Instructor: Wellness and Massage Training Institute. Former head of Chicago Bears' massage team.*

Do what you enjoy. Be the best at whatever you choose; prosperity follows quality and competence. When you focus on doing everything well, the money will take care of itself. For the opportunity to acquire knowledge or a new basic skill, I was glad to work for little pay. My worth is measured by how much I have learned as well as how much I have contributed.

Dick Green — *President/COO: Blistex, Incorporated. Member: Business Leaders for Excellence, Ethics, and Justice.*

I believe my mission on Earth is to do good; in return, I have been truly blessed and fortunate. In response to my many questions as a child, my relatives said, "Certainly you will be successful, because you already are!" There is no secret formula available for attaining success—just go with the flow of every opportunity. Also, learn as much as possible, display diligence in your work habits, maintain discipline, manage responsibilities, and stay focused. Give it your all and you will succeed.

Christiana Champ — *Master Shiatsu Therapist and Chinese Medicine Practitioner. Chi-Lel/Qigong Instructor.*

My success has been based on paying attention, listening to inner guidance, and following what was already planned for me. It has always been my heartfelt intention to meet God on the path. Acting in accordance with Divine Order, I show love and compassion for those around me. I feel like I have won the race when I am able to touch someone else's soul. Success is a built-in benefit, a great and most appreciated by-product.

Tom O'Donnell — *President/CEO: Full Circle Technologies. Past President: Kansas City Insurance Board.*

> It doesn't matter if you tee off with a putter;
> it's what you record on the scorecard.

Bernie Belkin — *Founder and CEO: Trans Continental, Inc. Director: Hi-tech investment group (Silicon Valley).*

During my teen years, using my musical abilities helped me to gain confidence and convinced me that I could excel. In my twenties, I heard the saying, "Take the middle road." I pride myself in always being able to do just that—balance family, friends, and career. It is my belief that this personal commitment also includes service and financial backing to community, country, and entire world. I invest my energy toward building a successful international network in which everyone wins.

Mary Jane Popp — *Host:* Poppoff *radio show. Actress, writer, former anchor of syndicated prime-time news.*

At twelve years old, I realized that I could make it on whatever God gave me. Really, He did give me a gift—the talent of being able to move people to tears and laughter with my singing and my words. Therefore, the stage is where I belong, and basically for all my life, that is where I have stayed.

Gaining knowledge from a variety of sources has been important to me. On my new radio show, I make it a top priority to interview many interesting guests from various fields. The information these professionals impart enables listeners to improve their lives. At the end of each program, I ask everyone to repeat three times, "Dare to dream, dare to dream, dare to dream." Never let go of that dream, for without a dream, you are without a life!

This book is about happiness, prosperity, and fulfillment. The key message to remember after reading _Angel First Aid_ is that you are really never alone while climbing the Steps to Success. Watch for synchronicity as it announces the close proximity of the Angels. When experiencing the blessings from these Celestial Beings, express your appreciation and be open to receiving more. The Angels want to make all things possible for you. Invite them into your life.

Glossary of Angels

Archangels

Gabriel, Angel of Communication: Delivers messages; works with the arts and invention.

Michael, Angel of Protection: Provides assistance and guidance; oversees divine justice.

Raphael, Angel of Healing: Creates strength and energy for well-being; promotes brotherhood.

Uriel, Angel of Spirituality: Inspires awareness as well as enlightenment; encourages prosperity.

Angel Specialists

Alan, Angel of Investments: Promotes financial growth; enhances sound decision-making.

Alexander, Angel of Invention: Cultivates ideas; inspires development of concepts.

Alicia, Angel of Serenity: Instills inner peace, harmony, and a sense of tranquility.

Allison, Angel of Plants: Supports the healthy growth or cultivation of plant life.

Annette, Angel of Gratitude: Encourages all appreciation and great thankfulness.

Barbara, Angel of Fame: Assists in career development of aspiring entertainers.

Barry, Angel of Strength: Increases energy for stamina; supplies power and support.

Bernard, Angel of Computers: Offers technical expertise, information, and skills.

Bettina, Angel of Creativity: Inspires new ideas for the arts, science, and business.

Blake, Angel of Comfort: Fosters physical well-being as well as peace of mind.

Brian, Angel of Relationships: Promotes harmonious and beneficial associations.

Calvin, Angel of Real Estate: Guides the acquisition or sale of real property.

Cameron, Angel of Weather: Protects throughout storms; oversees atmospheric conditions.

Caroline, Angel of Positive Thinking: Increases joyful, productive, uplifting thoughts.

Cheryl, Angel of Customer Relations: Fosters mutually beneficial, lucrative interactions.

Christopher, Angel of Opportunity: Opens all doors to successful business contacts.

Constance, Angel of Public Relations: Helps to generate influential media exposure.

Cornell, Angel of Decision-Making: Aids in an effective evaluation of information.

Cory, Angel of Career Development: Builds professional skills and solid opportunities.

Courtney, Angel of Responsibility: Organizes activities to complete tasks and duties.

Darrin, Angel of Housing: Helps to locate affordable and comfortable living space.

David, Angel of Camaraderie: Stimulates friendship for brotherhood and teamwork.

Deborah, Angel of Interviewing: Supplies support plus focus for job seekers.

Denice, Angel of Accounting: Compiles information and analyzes figures; manages finances.

Diane, Angel of Childcare: Connects children with able, loving, and reliable caregivers.

Douglas, Angel of Politics: Promotes credibility; retains relationships with constituents.

Eileen, Angel of Happiness: Instills a sense of well-being, contentment, and joy.

Esther, Angel of Vitality: Generates stamina, energy, and pep for vibrant health.

Evelyn, Angel of Manifesting: Attracts wealth, prosperity, success, and abundance.

Florence, Angel of Compassion: Encourages feelings of kindness, empathy, and concern.

Francis, Angel of Wisdom: Establishes a connection to higher guidance and understanding.

George, Angel of Success: Generates opportunities for prosperity and achievement.

Gordon, Angel of Focus: Increases concentration, clear thinking, and mental acuity.

Gunther, Angel of Fitness: Fortifies energy that helps with exercise routines.

Harold, Angel of Support: Locates beneficial mentors; offers guidance and security.

Irena, Angel of Patience: Improves ability to maintain composure and remain calm.

Jacob, Angel of Education: Expands comprehension as well as knowledge and awareness.

James, Angel of Public Speaking: Bolsters confidence; enhances people skills.

Jason, Angel of Organization: Supplies the focus needed to create order in thought or action.

Jeremiah, Angel of Financial Security: Helps to build a foundation for wealth.

Jessie, Angel of Deadlines: Offers support for completing assignments on time.

Joanne, Angel of Relaxation: Creates an atmosphere that encourages rest and recreation.

Jonathan, Angel of Business: Develops opportunities for companies to expand.

Jordan, Angel of Teamwork: Fosters camaraderie as well as support among colleagues.

Joseph, Angel of Joy: Bestows a sense of happiness, bliss, and real satisfaction.

Katrina, Angel of Prosperity: Assists in attainment of all health, wealth, and fulfillment.

Kevin, Angel of Friendship: Inspires affection, closeness, and mutual respect.

Kyle, Angel of Partnership: Promotes true compatibility; enhances beneficial associations.

Laramie, Angel of Discovery: Expedites prompt location of lost pets, objects, and people.

Leslie, Angel of Diplomacy: Advocates amicable business relationships and negotiations.

Lois, Angel of Clarity: Sharpens focus and understanding; stimulates much greater insight.

Lorena, Angel of Divine Grace: Delivers an abundance of spiritual blessings and enrichment.

Loretta, Angel of New Enterprise: Oversees all endeavors related to career and business.

Lucian, Angel of Resources: Creates many opportunities for prosperity and wealth.

Madeline, Angel of Teachers: Nurtures the capability to impart knowledge.

Marcus, Angel of Sales: Perfects selling techniques for profitable transactions.

Mariann, Angel of Efficiency: Maximizes productivity by enhancing focus and skill.

Marilyn, Angel of Leisure: Provides resources for play, fun, and relaxation.

Mary Jo, Angel of Print Media: Inspires creativity for successful journalistic efforts.

Maureen, Angel of Time: Assists with time management to complete projects.

Melody, Angel of Self-Esteem: Maintains internal belief in personal value and worth.

Melvin, Angel of Television: Cultivates ideas for content and production of programs.

Michelle, Angel of Radio Hosts: Improves the connection with the listening audience.

Mirra, Angel of Healing Arts: Promotes all modalities of healing; also offers compassion.

Nancy, Angel of Productivity: Initiates job performance and fosters efficiency.

Nicole, Angel of Negotiation: Directs all successful and satisfactory transactions.

Pamela, Angel of Environment: Encourages optimal life conditions for the planet.

Patrick, Angel of Sports: Coaches athletes for improved skill and performance.

Paula, Angel of Energy: Increases strength plus vitality for additional stamina.

Perrie, Angel of Music: Enhances abilities and talents by initiating musical expression.

Peter, Angel of Health: Cultivates wholeness, well-being, and dynamic energy.

Phillip, Angel of Employment: Sustains successful careers by finding suitable positions.

Rachel, Angel of Inspiration: Motivates with fresh ideas and uplifting, creative messages.

Randolph, Angel of Expansion: Arranges opportunities to increase business endeavors.

Raymond, Angel of Technology: Oversees operations of most electronic devices.

Rebecca, Angel of Confidence: Bolsters and strengthens a sense of self-esteem.

Rex, Angel of Cars: Works with mechanics to improve all automotive performance.

Rita, Angel of Writing: Clarifies thoughts; provides focus for creative expression.

Robert, Angel of Balance: Helps to achieve equilibrium, stability, and peace of mind.

Robin, Angel of Social Contact: Organizes events, dates, and gatherings with friends.

Ruth, Angel of Divine Justice: Settles disputes; provides equitable resolutions.

Sally, Angel of Perseverance: Bolsters persistence and the determination to achieve.

Samuel, Angel of Excellence: Enhances the desire to attain a high level of performance.

Sarah, Angel of Harmony: Promotes caring, peaceful, and balanced interactions.

Serena, Angel of Children: Nurtures, loves, and protects the young and young at heart.

Solomon, Angel of Security: Generates a sense of safety, stability, and well-being.

Susan, Angel of Travel: Sparks desire for adventure; also provides protection on trips.

Tara, Angel of Love: Delivers blessings for unconditional love, affection, and acceptance.

Terina, Angel of Attraction: Finds or connects soul mates; encourages compatibility.

Theodore, Angel of Kindness: Develops generosity and affection in relationships.

Theresa, Angel of Empowerment: Strengthens personal power and confidence.

Thomas, Angel of Animal Care: Provides protection plus healing and comfort to animals.

Timothy, Angel of Good Fortune: Generates abundance, wealth, and prosperity.

Trevor, Angel of Stocks: Guides market evaluation; also promotes investment success.

Tyler, Angel of Abundance: Supplies resources that bring financial blessings and security.

Ursula, Angel of Alignment: Affirms collaboration, sense of unity, and general accord.

Valerie, Angel of Understanding: Provides awareness or clarity and wisdom.

Victoria, Angel of Guidance: Shares advice and direction for additional support.

Walter, Angel of Banking: Manages financial transactions to increase net worth.

Wayne, Angel of Publishing: Ensures connection between authors and publishers.

William, Angel of Peace: Inspires serenity and tranquility; fosters union among nations.

Keys to Success

This index is a partial list of remedies that can be referenced by a keyword. Consider the ultimate outcome that you would expect to achieve. Look up the keyword that best describes the situation or solution. Then, select the most appropriate remedy.

*Best one to use.

Keyword	Remedy	Page
Athletics	*Instant Replay	76
	Confidence Builder	77
	Energy Ball	85
	Go for the Gold	53
	Solid Foundation	92
	Twisting	84
Balance	*Creative Colors	60
	Angelic Choir	44
	Breathing Technique	21
	Coffee Break	45
	Serenity Float	43
	Vitality Plus	83
Business	*Vision Statement	27
	Climb to Success	99
	Expand Your Territory	100
	Law of Increase	52
	Sales for Success	91
	Wealth Affirmation	76
Career	*Career Bliss	68
	Business Honors	93
	Confidence Builder	77
	Meeting an Angel	91
	Taking Inventory	28
	Yes or No	35
Clarity	*Voice Mail	59
	Angelic Solution	68
	Baroque Beat	29
	Break Room	43
	Coffee Break	45
	Serenity Float	43

Keyword	Remedy	Page
Communication	*Meeting an Angel*	91
	Follow Through	36
	Morale Booster	67
	Negotiating Angels	60
	Serenity Float	43
	Voice Mail	59
Confidence	*Go for the Gold*	53
	Climb to Success	99
	Confidence Builder	77
	Instant Replay	76
	Shower of Money	101
	The Judge	75
Courage	*Morale Booster*	67
	Breathing Technique	21
	Bridge to Success	59
	Energy Ball	85
	Goal Setting	27
	Power Surge	51
Creativity	*Picture of Success*	67
	Academic Excellence	75
	Creative Colors	60
	Instant Replay	76
	Power Coins	84
	Vision Statement	27
Criticism (overcoming)	*The Judge*	75
	Angelic Choir	44
	Bridge to Success	59
	Confidence Builder	77
	Creative Colors	60
	Energy Ball	85

Keyword	Remedy	Page
Education	*Academic Excellence*	75
	Baroque Beat	29
	Piece by Piece	35
	School of Success	100
	Solid Foundation	92
	Time Prosperity	36
Empowerment	*Power Surge*	51
	Backbone	51
	Confidence Builder	77
	Energy Ball	85
	Go for the Gold	53
	Shower of Money	101
Energy	*Vitality Plus*	83
	Backbone	51
	Confidence Builder	77
	Energy Ball	85
	Power Surge	51
	Twisting	84
Enlightenment	*Break Room*	43
	Angelic Solution	68
	Coffee Break	45
	Creative Colors	60
	Serenity Float	43
	Voice Mail	59
Enthusiasm	*Twisting*	84
	Energy Tap	83
	Law of Increase	52
	Money Magnet	99
	Solid Foundation	92
	Vision Statement	27

Keyword	Remedy	Page
Expansion	*Expand Your Territory*	100
	Law of Increase	52
	Picture of Success	67
	Time Prosperity	36
	Vision Statement	27
	Wealth Affirmation	76
Fear (overcoming)	*Bridge to Success*	59
	Angelic Solution	68
	Baroque Beat	29
	Breathing Technique	21
	Confidence Builder	77
	The Judge	75
Financial Security	*Money Magnet*	99
	Banking Cash	61
	Easy Money	44
	Law of Increase	52
	Shower of Money	101
	Wealth Affirmation	76
Focus	*Baroque Beat*	29
	Brain Fog	28
	Picture of Success	67
	Taking Inventory	28
	Time Prosperity	36
	Voice Mail	59
Fun	*Play Money*	92
	Energy Ball	85
	Instant Replay	76
	Money Magnet	99
	Morale Booster	67
	Voice Mail	59

Keyword	Remedy	Page
Growth	*Law of Increase	52
	Career Bliss	68
	Confidence Builder	77
	Expand Your Territory	100
	Sales for Success	91
	The Judge	75
Happiness	*Bridge to Success	59
	Angel Scrapbook	22
	Break Room	43
	Go for the Gold	53
	Play Money	92
	Serenity Float	43
Harmony	*Creative Colors	60
	Angelic Choir	44
	Baroque Beat	29
	Break Room	43
	Coffee Break	45
	Serenity Float	43
Health	*Vitality Plus	83
	Breathing Technique	21
	Bridge to Success	59
	Confidence Builder	77
	Energy Ball	85
	Twisting	84
Inner Peace	*Coffee Break	45
	Angelic Choir	44
	Breathing Technique	21
	Creative Colors	60
	Energy Ball	85
	Serenity Float	43

Keyword	Remedy	Page
Interviewing	*Confidence Builder*	77
	Brain Fog	28
	Breathing Technique	21
	Career Bliss	68
	Go for the Gold	53
	Meeting an Angel	91
Life's Purpose	*Angel Scrapbook*	22
	Break Room	43
	Coffee Break	45
	School of Success	100
	Voice Mail	59
	Yes or No	35
Money	*Money Magnet*	99
	Bank Rolls	52
	Banking Cash	61
	Dollar Signs	69
	Play Money	92
	Power Coins	84
Morale	*Morale Booster*	67
	Climb to Success	99
	Go for the Gold	53
	School of Success	100
	Solid Foundation	92
	Twisting	84
Negativity (overcoming)	*Angelic Solution*	68
	Backbone	51
	Bridge to Success	59
	Go for the Gold	53
	Solid Foundation	92
	The Judge	75

Keyword	Remedy	Page
Productivity	*Follow Through*	36
	Expand Your Territory	100
	Picture of Success	67
	Piece by Piece	35
	Solid Foundation	92
	Time Prosperity	36
Prosperity	*Money Magnet*	99
	Bank Rolls	52
	Law of Increase	52
	Power Coins	84
	Shower of Money	101
	Wealth Affirmation	76
Relaxation	*Serenity Float*	43
	Angelic Choir	44
	Baroque Beat	29
	Breathing Technique	21
	Coffee Break	45
	Creative Colors	60
Responsibility	*Piece by Piece*	35
	Career Bliss	68
	Follow Through	36
	Solid Foundation	92
	Taking Inventory	28
	Time Prosperity	36
Strength	*Power Surge*	51
	Backbone	51
	Confidence Builder	77
	Energy Ball	85
	Instant Reply	76
	Vitality Plus	83

Contacting The Angel Lady

**Calls for consultations, speaking
engagements, and interviews
are always welcome.**

Angelight Productions
**1038 Whirlaway Avenue
Naperville, IL 60540
800-323-1790
630-420-1334
630-420-1474 (Fax)
suestorm@earthlink.net
www.theangellady.net**

**When sending e-mail,
please include phone number.**